A SPARK FROM HEAVEN?

The Place of Potential in Organizational and Individual Development

Adrian W. Savage

PNA Publishing
New Jersey, USA

Text © Copyright Adrian W. Savage, 2002
ISBN 0-9718369-0-6

All rights reserved. No part of this publication may be reproduced, distributed, or transmitted in any form or by any means, including photocopying, recording, or other electronic or mechanical methods, without the prior written permission of the publisher; except in the case of brief quotations embodied in critical reviews and certain other noncommercial uses permitted by copyright law.

Published by PNA Publishing
1130 Route 202 South
Raritan, New Jersey 08869
www.nettps.com

First Edition
ISBN   0-9718369-0-6

10 9 8 7 6 5 4 3 2 1

Printed in the United States of America

ACKNOWLEDGEMENTS

Like all books, this has been a collaborative effort. Without the encouragement of Martine Berreiter, I would probably never have started, let alone finished. She has handled all the technical aspects of publishing, as well as providing me with constant, gentle urging to get along and finish. I am truly grateful.

Brenda Nashawaty gave me much needed encouragement when it mattered. She read through several proofs and never lost faith in the project, even when I did.

Laura Harris has contributed her outstanding talent by designing the beautiful cover.

Beverly Kaye provided unstinting backing at the crucial moment when the writing was all but finished and I was beginning to wish I had never started. At that point, I think she believed in me much more than I believed in myself.

Most of all, I wish to thank Marion, my wife of twenty seven years, without whose love and unquestioning support my life would have been entirely lacking in any kind of potential.

Needless to say, any mistakes are entirely down to me.

Adrian Savage
New Jersey, 2002

CONTENTS

PREFACE	1
WHAT IS POTENTIAL?	7
STARTING OUT	17
Imaginary boundaries	19
Responsible versus accountable	20
Deficit thinking	22
Focusing on gifts	25
AWARENESS	29
Potential as a process	31
Quick fixes do not work	35
CONSCIOUS CHOICES	39
Cause and effect	43
Awareness and conscious choice	44
Data, information and knowledge	46
STRENGTHS AND VALUES	51
Watching ourselves	53
How is more important than *what*	55
Kick-starting the process	56
Where do we fit best?	58
MOTIVATIONS, EMOTIONS AND REASON	61
Matters of the heart	65
Unconscious values	67
Habitual thinking	69
Paths to learning	71

FAITH IN THE JOURNEY 75
The importance of faith 76
Going it alone 79

POSTCARDS 83
Does it align with our core values? 84
Does it feel exciting? 87
Does it build on our strengths? 88
Is this a stretch? 90
Is it increasing our learning? 92
Are we learning something, not about something? 93
Does it broaden minds and open perspectives? 94
Does it produce more value, confidence or joy? 96

BLOCKAGES AND ANTIDOTES 99
Letting go of negative beliefs 101
Dealing with anger 103
The trap of jealousy 106
Conquering self-loathing 108

WHEN STRENGTHS WORK AGAINST US 111
Deteriorated strengths 113
Spotting dysfunctional values 115
Diversity 118
Restoring our strengths 120
Shifting focus 121
"Zooming" 122

THE ART OF POSSIBILITY 125
Rule Number 6 126
The gift of uncertainty 127
A universe of possibilities 130
The power of probing questions 133
The importance of not knowing 135
Living on the edge 137

WHY SPOIL THE HABITS OF A LIFETIME? ... 141
    Stepping beyond our habits 145
    Flying on automatic pilot 148

YOU ARE WHAT YOU CHOOSE 153
    Missing the momentous choices 158

CONCEPTS AND TOOLKITS 165
    Attention! Attention! 167
    An imaginary world of scarcity 169
    Building your toolkit 173
    Responses versus reactions 177

CONSCIOUS INCOMPETENCE 181
    Practicing conscious incompetence 184
    Mentors as protectors 186

THE EVEN BIGGER PICTURE 191
    Multiple contexts 194
    Creating perspective 196
    Contexts and opportunities 197
    Distinguishing causes from effects 200
    Dealing with dilemmas 202
    Real transformation 204

SELECT BIBLIOGRAPHY 207

PREFACE

> Thou waitest for the spark from heaven and we,
>   Light half-believers of our casual creeds,
>   Who never deeply felt, nor clearly will'd,
> Whose insight never has borne fruit in deeds,
> Whose vague resolves never have been fulfill'd;
>   For whom each year we see
> Breeds new beginnings, disappointments new;
>   Who hesitate and falter life away,
> And lose tomorrow the ground won today—
>   Ah! Do not we, wanderer, await it too?
>   MATTHEW ARNOLD, "THE SCHOLAR GYPSY"

Although I did not know it at the time, I grew up with a huge advantage over many other children: the assurance that I had abundant potential waiting to be used. None of the adults around me ever suggested I should be satisfied with anything less than excellence, or that I had any natural limitations that would hold me back. Their confidence became mine and I faced each challenge knowing I had what was needed to deal with it.

Yet I had no privileged childhood. My father left school aged fourteen and spent more than thirty years in the same job, rising eventually to first-line supervisor. Later, when I began working, my first salary was greater than he had ever earned. My mother took various jobs in local stores to help supplement the family budget.

We lived in an extended family over a small clothing shop in an ancient but obscure city in the west of England. My great-uncle owned the shop. It sold basic clothing on simple credit terms to people whose income in that farming community was far below that of the factory workers in larger towns. People paid a fixed sum every week and could take credit up to a multiple of that amount. Payments were often collected in person by two elderly men who went around the town on bicycles.

Somehow, money was found to give my sister and me a good education, supplemented by scholarships. She was the first member of our whole family to go to a university. I was the second.

Later, when my great uncle became too infirm at nearly eighty years old to run the shop, he sold it and we moved to a middle class suburban house with a large garden, in which my father grew vegetables and wonderful flowers and worked in his greenhouse.

Throughout this time, I was never hampered by people who doubted that I had ability. I did well at school and then at university. Was this a genetic gift? If it was, I have no idea from where it came. All my family, for many generations, had been humble agricultural workers. No one had ever, as far as I know, either shown academic talent or desired it.

Now, when I look back, I can see the enormity of the gift I was given. Nobody stood in my way. Inspired by their confidence, I did not block my own progress either. What potential I had was allowed full expression, within the bounds of a small provincial town. It never occurred to me that anything could limit my progress except my own determination and courage. My sister and I both flourished and found our paths in life. No gift could have been greater.

POTENTIAL is widely discussed yet even more widely misunderstood. People make potential in the workplace sound rare and mysterious, something that belongs only to special people. This is not true. We all have potential. It is so common that most of us have more than we know how to use and do not appreciate how to connect with it. We are often bored and cynical at work because we know we are settling for less that we want or deserve. Yet we still do not grasp clearly what to do about it.

How has potential gained this mystique? When told it is rare, we believe what we are told. We are convinced that it is a wary beast which must be hunted with skill and care. "Not enough of it around," we are told. "Have to try to get our share." So organizations establish fast-track programs and try to snare high-potential staff before competitors snap them up. Should we capture some of these almost mythical beasts, we may kill them with kindness or find they are not as wonderful as we had hoped. Some prove their worth, others disappoint. They are only human after all. Nobody told us that we would probably have found the same potential amongst the people we already employ. Our search has probably been wasted, at least in part.

Like many good things, potential was appropriated for centuries by the rich and powerful. They have quietly been farming it through expensive private schools and exclusive universities; monopolizing these sources for their own benefit. For decades, everyone denied the disgraceful notion that potential could exist in minority groups, such as women, or races other than white ones. Sadly, some people still believe it to be true.

Belief in a spark from heaven is a false belief. No miraculous talent needs to descend on us to make us into someone worthwhile. We are already worthwhile, all of us. To be sure, we have differing talents and differing levels of determination to turn those talents into actuality. Diversity is part of the natural scheme of things. We are the ones who give some arbitrary value to the talents around us, praising some and neglecting others. This book, I hope, will show that all our gifts are of equal value, since they make us what and who we are.

In the poem that opens this book, Matthew Arnold, who was an eminent scholar and headmaster of one of England's finest schools during the nineteenth century, expresses the fears and disappointments many of us have felt. It is easy to be overwhelmed by all our false starts and broken dreams. We envy those who seem to have everything without visible effort. We convince ourselves that without a spark from heaven things will continue much as they are: confusing, uncertain and often far less than we desire.

Reality is all these things. Reality is also the people who rise to greatness from the most terrible beginnings. Reality is the millions of people who live satisfying and enjoyable lives, however imperfect. Reality is the teacher who inspires a generation of young people, the nurse who brings comfort and reassurance to people terrified by their own pain, and the entrepreneur who creates work and prospects for a community.

A SPARK FROM HEAVEN?

I want to show you that we all have potential and can use it to make our own lives better and benefit all those we contact each day. We have no need of a spark from heaven or, if such a thing exists, we have it already. All we need to do is step out of our own way and allow our natural gifts to grow as they were meant to do.

ONE

WHAT IS POTENTIAL?

> It is a most mortifying reflection for a man to consider what he has done, compared to what he might have done.
>
> SAMUEL JOHNSON

> Knowledge of what is possible is the beginning of happiness.
>
> SANTAYANA

Potential is very simple. *It is a deliberate choice to undertake something more demanding than we are doing right now, allied with the opportunity or possibility to make such a change.* Potential does not just mean having the drive and determination to become a top executive. Such narrow, elitist definitions exclude the overwhelming majority of people, as maybe they are designed to do, and convince them that they have no potential worth cultivating. Nothing could be further from the truth.

The old argument about nature versus nurture as the basis for our lives can also be laid to rest. Both are necessary and neither is useful without the other. Nature — our genetic inheritance — is like the flame that lights a fire. Without its presence there is no combustion. Yet the eventual size and heat of the fire depends on how it is nurtured once alight: what it is fed and the conditions in which the fire burns. Damp conditions with insufficient kindling will never produce a healthy blaze, regardless of the power of the initial flame.

This is good news. Whether our own initial flame is large or small, we can build a good blaze by careful feeding with the appropriate kinds of fuel. Some organizations begin with ideas or products that seem sure-fire winners, but the environment is damp and unfriendly to burning; or the managers in charge feed their own egos and bank accounts instead of the fire the organization needs. Other companies seem to have little to commend them at the start, yet go on to build massive, blazing success. What we pay attention to and feed will usually grow, given a modestly suitable environment. What we neglect will smolder and die, even in the most suitable context.

You will find four things in this book:
1. How to understand the true nature of potential, at least in that part of life devoted to work.
2. Where to find potential and how to recognize it.
3. How to access those talents and possibilities that are not yet realized and use them to boost performance and productivity.
4. How to direct future events into positive and fruitful directions.

Most of us have been brought up on the idea that potential is something you either have or you do not. The definitions of potential put about by many organizations convince many people that they do not have any. These definitions are mostly bunkum with little or no relevance to people's likely behaviors in the real world. Many are impossible ideals dreamed up by people with time on their hands and overheated imaginations.

POTENTIAL is just a word that we use as a placeholder for all the things that you and I *could* do but have not yet done. Generally, we either passed these things by because of lack of opportunity, or thoughtless choices, or ignorance of the possibilities. Many have not even occurred yet in our lives. It is *always* expansive: it opens our minds to new ideas, adds to our skills and experiences and broadens our viewpoints and perspectives. In contrast, much of what we do without thinking each day constricts our minds. We narrow down our thoughts, using old habits to exclude possibilities that do not fit with our preconceptions and opinions. We create rules for ourselves that state what we can and cannot do. We ignore our own gifts and abilities or crave skills we do not possess. In the process we make ourselves miserable and frustrated.

We cannot know what will come about in our lives. The future is always less certain than we hope or wish. Sudden changes in direction can – and probably will – happen to all of us. Most of life is a process of adaptation and improvisation: doing the best we can and managing to cope despite lacking the knowledge, skills or preparation we would have chosen, had we only known what we would have to face.

This process of adapting and improvising is the seed bed of potential. Without it, we would simply repeat ourselves. No learning would take place beyond formal classroom teaching. No one would display truly surprising talents – astonishing themselves as much as others. Over the millennia, our whole species has been shaped by the need to cope with the unexpected.

Adaptability, innovation and improvisation sum up true potential well. It is that will and activity needed to rise to unknown challenges as they occur. It is always active, reaching forward to cope with life's uncertainties instead of trying to ignore them or run away from them.

The key to developing potential – the subject matter of this book – can also be found in improvisation. Those who improvise for a living, like jazz players, know that the wider their basic repertoire, the better their improvisations will be. We need something to improvise *from*: some basis of knowledge, skill and experience that can allow us to innovate and find new ways forward. Improvisation cannot happen in a vacuum.

As we learn and improvise, if we are wise, we increase our repertoire. Nothing is wasted. It is only our rooted attachment to repeating the habits of our past that continually interferes with this natural process of accessing and developing potential.

It is tempting to think that potential is either based on things in our past — the age-old idea that history repeats itself — or that it lies somewhere unknown in the future. Since the past is history and the future is a mystery, neither seems a good place to look for potential. No one, so far as I know, has succeeded in changing the past, just as no one has managed to predict the future accurately and precisely — despite the massive resources that Wall Street applies to this fruitless task. If the army of statisticians, analysts and assorted pundits assembled in the stock markets of the world cannot predict what a simple thing like a stock price will be next week, there is not much hope that we can tell what our lives will be like in two or three or ten years time. We need to be able to find our potential in the present.

SOME OF THE most highly respected leaders in history seemed to be failures at some point in their lives. What prevented them from going to the grave without revealing anything of their true potential was the luck of being in the right place at the right time. In more than thirty years of working with some pretty smart people, from nuclear scientists to venture capitalists, I've seen for myself how much potential is blocked by simple things like ignorance, unexamined habits and untested opinions. I do not claim to write from a theoretical position or academic standpoint. This book is based on my own experience. Everything has been tried and tested and verified in the real world. It is a record of what I have seen and heard and come slowly to understand.

We all prefer good news, so in case you have some niggling fear that you may not have the potential you wish to have, let us get something straight at the outset. You have no way of knowing what your potential will be unless you take the trouble to find out. Sir Winston Churchill is remembered by history as a magnificent orator and an inspirational leader in Britain's darkest hours of World War II. Yet before he became prime minister (at an age when most people would be retiring from work) he was generally regarded as a failure — a maverick politician who had deserted his party more than once, held some senior posts without much distinction and generally frittered away his opportunities. Even in war, his track record was bad. The disastrous Dardanelles Expedition he championed in World War I cost thousands of Allied lives and ended in ignominious defeat by the Turkish Army. When he was finally given the chance to lead Britain as prime minister — and then only when the 'sensible' policies of his predecessor had failed utterly — Churchill revealed talents that no one at the time would have believed he had. As Stephen Bungay writes:[1]

> The weaknesses which had kept Churchill out of power for so long were precisely the strengths which brought him into power on 10 May [1940]. He was not a pragmatist, but a visionary. His vision was intuitive, inspiring and uncannily accurate. For years, he had been using melodramatic rhetoric that seemed hopelessly out of touch with reality. Churchill remained stubbornly true to his convictions and said what he had always said. Slowly at first, then rapidly and suddenly, reality raised itself up to be worthy of him.

There will always be people who claim to know what is going to happen, and who will make it and who will not. We have all encountered wiseacres who tell us we will never be worth anything. It is important to see these prophesies for what they are — just opinions, with no special claim to truth and therefore no particular importance.

LET US AGREE that potential consists of all the gifts we could be using and the things we could be doing, or thinking, or saying, or learning, but have not yet done, thought,

---

[1] Bungay, Stephen, **The Most Dangerous Enemy: A History of the Battle of Britain**. London: Aurum Press, 2000.

said or learned — and leave it at that. It is much more useful to explore potential than waste time on definitions. Realizing potential takes purposeful *action today*, not definitions — so let us get on with it.

Where do we start? Right where we are. There is nowhere else. If we put off the chance to realize our potential until we are in a better place — or a better time — we will probably never begin. There is no better place to start than where we are and no better time than today.

We have what we have, so we need to work out how to make the best use of whatever knowledge, skills and experience we already possess, especially any gifts we are not using. Start finding ways of putting them to use. So many of us refuse to see the options that are right in front of us. Instead, we stare into the distance somewhere, fixing our hopes and dreams on possibilities that are remote or unlikely. Begin with the talents and skills you have already and work with whatever advantages you possess. Do not ignore your gifts or spend your time wishing you had others.

If we are not actively involved in creating the ways in which our lives will unfold, they will develop without us. Others will construct the plot of our personal life history — friends, family, employers, supporters and enemies. Their plots for our lives will not be what *we* want to achieve, but what *they* want us to do. Mostly, these plots are stereotyped and hackneyed — do what you are told and do not cause trouble.

If we hand over our lives to chance, like leaves in the autumn wind, we will go where the next event pushes us, whether we like it or not. Some courage is essential to begin the journey towards realizing our potential. It is not an exotic kind of bravery. We need only the simple determination to write our own script and chose consciously how we will adapt to life's challenges and opportunities. We cannot know in advance what we will face, so we must often improvise or muddle through in whatever way we can. That is how we learn, if we are wise. That is how we build a life we can look back on with pride – and often with humor.

Trusting in fate, or in the choices others make for us, will never build us into fully functioning human beings, let alone draw out the potential we have within us. We are either the authors of our own story or the cardboard characters in someone else's.

Our potential is that story waiting to be told, full of vivid incidents and heart-pounding action. Like all good stories, there will be many twists and turns along the way; moments of elation and times of near despair. Some stories will echo through the corridors of power and some will be known only to a few ordinary people. But however the story ends, it will be ours: unique, irreplaceable and never to be repeated in the whole vast history of the universe.

Summary

* Potential is the willingness and deliberate choice to undertake something more demanding than we are doing right now, allied with the opportunity or possibility to make such a change.
* Potential is possibility and is *always* expansive: it opens our minds to new ideas, adds to our skills and experiences and broadens viewpoints and perspec-

tives. In contrast, much of what we do without thinking each day constricts our potential.
- Adaptability, improvisation and openness to change are the bedrock on which potential is founded. Without them, little will be realized.
- Realizing potential takes purposeful *action today*.
- Begin with the gifts, skills and advantages you have already. Do not spend time wishing you had others.
- Unless we are actively working to create the ways in which our lives will unfold, they will develop without us.

TWO

STARTING OUT

> Do what you can, with what you have, where you are.
>
> — THEODORE ROOSEVELT

> Life would be infinitely happier if we could only be born at the age of eighty and gradually approach eighteen.
>
> — MARK TWAIN

Preparing for a journey is usually a good idea. It helps to get things into the right perspective. This is where we will be heading and what we will be hoping to find:

* A way to discover potential in ourselves and in our teams and organizations, and to describe it in practical terms, so that we can decide how to use these opportunities to increase our productivity and satisfaction.
* The links between cause and effect which will allow us to influence future outcomes.

* How to be more skillful in our actions and dealings with others.

More people have the aspiration to access potential than succeed. There are many reasons, some springing from questions and fears about the process itself.

* Can we really bring about change in our organizations and working lives?
* What will it take? Is it within *our* power to achieve?
* What results can we expect? Will they be worth the effort?

These are the basic assumptions behind the work we need to do to realize personal and organizational potential:

* In nearly all situations, something works. Do not waste time wishing things were different. Where we are is where we start. Build on what works already.
* What we focus on expands and grows. Focusing on gifts expands them. Focusing on weaknesses makes us weaker, more miserable and less able to cope.
* Our choices, whether they are made consciously or not, always affect our future. Making choices consciously is common sense.
* Potential is always expansive, adding to options, broadening viewpoints and increasing competence.
* Automatic habits are constrictive. They close us down, narrow our options and limit our perspectives. They encourage us to repeat the past, whether or not it still works for us. If we carry parts of ourselves into the future, they should only be the best parts.
* Potential is not fixed. It arises where present and future possibilities intersect with the willingness and skill to choose between them.

* Improvising is the sure sign of potential on the move. It is not indicative of some lack of basic ability. Not knowing is a better place to begin than assuming we know and being proven wrong.

Imaginary boundaries

Perhaps we have come to believe all this talk of accessing potential is not practical. To keep our jobs, we have to do what others want. There is a great deal of truth in this objection. We are not free agents. We must comply with certain rules and expectations, whether we agree with them or not. Other people do not usually have our wishes at the top of their agendas. Those who pay the piper expect to call the tune and feel justified in criticizing how we play.

Yet if we look deeper, we will see a critical fallacy. The unspoken logic is, "Because we cannot have everything we want, we cannot have *anything*." We must accept that life will not always turn out exactly as we want. That is the way it is. It does not mean we have to become fatalists and accept whatever comes along. We can still influence what happens, even if we cannot control things totally. There is a close link between our past choices and the results we get today, so how we act now will certainly influence the future.

In the nineteenth century, Carl Benz, the pioneer of gasoline powered vehicles, was powerless to stop the local authority in his area passing a by-law preventing the dangerous new horseless carriages from going faster than walking speed. His vehicles could easily go much quicker, but the law was the law. He did not relish selling expensive machines that offered no speed advantage over using your own feet, so he seized his chance to influence events when a government minister visited the city.

Benz invited the minister for a drive and arranged for the local milkman to come behind with his horse-drawn milk cart. The milkman did not have to obey the speed limit, so he quickly overtook Benz and the minister and disappeared ahead. The minister was furious at being passed by a milkman and demanded Benz go faster. Benz explained the local speed law. It was quickly repealed.

Responsible versus accountable

We are rarely directly *responsible* for what happens to us, but we are always *accountable* for our responses to events. Responsibility means causing something to happen. Events for which we are truly responsible are few. Most things come about whether we do anything or not. We have not caused them to occur. Chance, world economic trends, other people's actions, political interference or some natural disaster play havoc with our plans.

Being accountable means accepting that we can *choose* our responses to events. Before you object that we are not free here either, given all the duties, obligations, laws, regulations and expectations that hem us in, stop and think. It may be unpleasant, or difficult, or disadvantageous to say no. But there are very, very few situations — if any at all — where it is truly impossible. We always have at least one choice, though it may be a bitter one. In this book, there are two themes: awareness and conscious choice which go together and strengthen each other. Both require that we accept full accountability for much of what happens in our lives.

If we hold to the view that what happens is outside our control, awareness is not necessary. It might be better to be drugged into insensibility. At least we would be spared the fear of seeing bad things coming and believing we are helpless to turn them away. Choice, conscious or otherwise, is irrelevant if the future is either random or completely predestined.

Accepting our accountability does not mean we do not need help from others. We need their perceptions and responses to gauge the effect of what we do: whether or not we are skillful in bringing about the results we intend. We need their support and encouragement. We are all connected to one another through a web of relatedness. Even so, we are still accountable for our own actions: what we do, say, or believe is up to us.

IN ANCIENT GREEK mythology, Oedipus seems at first to be an innocent victim, cursed at birth by an especially unpleasant prophecy. He is abandoned to die as soon as he is born, because his family has been told he is destined to murder his father and marry his mother: a mixture of patricide and incest that would cause the writers of today's supermarket tabloids to offer him a vast advance for his story.

A kindly old couple rescues baby Oedipus and raises him as their own son. But when he grows up, he has grand ideas and is not content to act like a proper peasant. He wants to seek his fortune in the big city. So he journeys to Thebes and everything happens exactly as the prophecy foretold. Stricken with remorse, Oedipus blinds himself. Notice that he does not offer excuses or explain that he did not know the man he met and killed on his way was his father; nor does he point out that the strangely attractive older woman he married on his arrival in the city did not tell him she was his mother — because, of course, neither of them knew.

He accepts his accountability and punishment. Sophocles, who wrote a fine tragedy about Oedipus, clearly agreed that this was just. So did the audience for the play. Why?

Oedipus did not have to kill the man on the road. He felt he had been insulted, lost his temper and lashed out. Prophecy or no prophecy, this was not an action he could pass off as due to anyone else. Later he knew that by marrying the dead man's wife he would become king, and he really wanted that. He had just solved the riddle of the Sphinx — a murderously tricky female — and he was feeling pleased with himself. He thought he deserved the throne, so when the grateful citizens suggested he take it, plus the newly widowed queen as part of a package deal, he accepted. Oedipus was not responsible for the options that fate and the gods put before him, but he never doubted that he was fully accountable for all his actions. As Jerry Harvey points out in his management meditations, whenever we find we have been stabbed in the back, our own fingerprints are always on the knife.[2]

Deficit thinking

One of the principal reasons behind our fear of accepting accountability is the habit of looking for gaps and deficiencies in ourselves, in those around us and in our work. Our glasses are always half empty, never half full.

---

[2] See Select Bibliography under Jerry B. Harvey, 1999.

A SPARK FROM HEAVEN?

We put up protective walls of opinions, prejudices, attitudes and emotions to help us feel secure and avoid the discomfort of risking something new and untried.

I am not sure how or why this situation arose. Perhaps we cling to the idea that medicine will not work if it does not taste dreadful. Perhaps we believe we have to feel the pain of our inadequacy to get the gain of doing better. Perhaps it stems from pessimists who believe that human beings are hopelessly lazy and never willingly make any effort. They must be frightened or shamed into action by having their weaknesses and imperfections revealed in grisly detail.

Advertising is another influence. Frightening customers into buying is a common sales technique. Sales people suggest customers are missing something everyone else has; use research to invent an industry standard and show how people fall short; or make it look as if organizations contain glaring deficiencies that your product happens to deal with. It is not true that sex is the most common way to sell products. It is really fear, including the fear of not being sexy enough.

We have incorporated this sales technique into our cultural beliefs about our world and have been trained to look for gaps in order to fill them. The habit is so bad that some of us will not take action unless we can *prove* there is a gap to be filled.

This attitude is common in business. An organization creates a notional gap in its sales by making a voluntary statement, called a budget or forecast, that sales will be X percent higher by the end of the next period. Now it acts to fill the gap as if there was a *real* shortfall, not one caused by its own declaration. If the imagined shortfall is

23

not met, there is trouble and people are blamed or punished. Stock market analysts create expectations about some company's future profits and then respond with shock and panic selling if these expectations are not met.

We take opinions for reality, thoughts for truth, and ideas as real problems. What if those opinions and thoughts were simply wrong and the gaps never existed outside our own minds? If we assume a gap or a deficit exists, it does. But if we question it, it may disappear.

I worked for many years as a consultant to an engineering company that took the deficit approach to extremes. Senior managers would tell you, with pride, that it was their policy to avoid all surprises. If results fell below the budget, the people responsible were judged incompetent and punished. If managers exceeded their budget, it was assumed they had either lied about business progress or proved to be incompetent planners. So they were also punished. Everyone's results came in exactly on target, whatever odd accounting that took to achieve. In that company, playing safe was the only game in town.

There is nothing wrong with setting targets. The mischief comes when we believe our creations are real, seeing a deficiency where a gap exists only because we tell ourselves that it does. Managers often try to convince subordinates of the need for improvement by elaborating on their deficiencies. But criticism creates fear and antagonism. We quickly learn to sit and listen outwardly, while raging inside. The desire to improve comes from feeling valued for what you do and wishing to be valued more highly in future if you can do better. Praise raises spirits. Blame only raises hackles.

A SPARK FROM HEAVEN?

Focusing on gifts

The finest antidote to criticism and our imaginary fears about our potential is to focus on our personal and organizational gifts. We all have gifts of some kind. We can see what use we can make of them in our work, instead of being fooled by fear that our gifts are not special enough. Every gift can be made into something worthwhile. Looking for positives is the only course that makes sense. Forget gaps and weaknesses. Everyone has them. They are nothing special. Gifts, however, may be very special indeed.

Imagine a cook who has been asked to prepare a meal in a hurry in a strange kitchen. He goes to the cupboards to see what ingredients are available. Perhaps they are quite basic: rice, a few vegetables, some spices. A thoughtful cook can make a memorable meal with those. If the cupboards are full of exotic things — caviar, fine chocolate, oysters and French cheeses — a good cook can use those too. But a poor, thoughtless cook could no more make a fine meal from exotic ingredients than from plain ones. In fact, a meal with rare, expensive ingredients could well be worse. Handling rich foods and flavors takes skill if the goal is not to produce nausea.

We all have gifts and abilities. Some things work for us. If we focus our attention on deficits and gaps, on our weaknesses, they will expand until they become great chasms that we cannot cross. If we focus on our strengths, they will grow into greater ones.

WE LIVE WITHIN a huge field of possibilities yet only use a small part of this field because we are seeking the illusion of security. We believe we will be safest by relying on old habits. Habits let us feel comfortable, but also keep us from extending ourselves into other parts of the field. Remember that the field of untapped potential lies where the possibilities available encounter the willingness and capacity to take advantage of them. That means that people who extend their capacity and motivation extend their potential as well. Whether we take care with decisions or throw them off hastily, relying on our personal automatic pilot — our ingrained habits. So we mostly get what we choose, even though we may not have chosen consciously.

Once we have formed habits — as we all do — we carry them with us wherever we go, not recognizing we have brought them along. Poor or unskillful habits from our past swiftly ruin our ability to build a successful future. Give up blaming others for the way life turns out. Even if this sometimes feels justifiable, it is never helpful. Instead, understand clearly what you are carrying. Sort through your passengers and eject any who are no longer assets.

Summary

* Potential is a pattern of possibilities and options. It does not operate in the real world until we act on options to make them real or let them pass away.
* Every action counts whether it is conscious or not. What matters is recognizing the need to choose and ensuring each choice is made consciously.
* We must subject everything we find — or are told — to careful investigation. Do not be fooled by appearances. Go beyond opinions and ideas to find what is real.
* These are the essential steps on any journey towards exploring and realizing potential:

1. Acceptance of full accountability for progress — or lack of it — towards using all your natural gifts to benefit others as well as yourself.
2. The resolve to set out with confidence on the journey to finding our true potential.
3. Exploring avidly to discover the directions that best fit our characters and interests as they develop.
4. Giving our attention to activities that expand our horizons and increase our options. That is where we will find most potential.
5. Recognizing where unconscious habits are blocking our way forward and finding ways to step around them. Resistance to attempts to limit us and hem us in.
6. The resolve to keep on doing this for the rest of our working lives and beyond.

THREE

AWARENESS

> How many people eat, drink and get married; buy, sell and build; make contracts and attend to their fortune; have friends and enemies, pleasures and pains, are born, grow up, live and die — but asleep!
>
> — JOSEPH JOUBERT

> Fate is non-awareness.
>
> — JAN KOTT

Over the entrance to the ancient temple at Delphi, in Greece, where the Delphic Oracle was consulted by kings, generals, wise men and anxious politicians, two words in Ancient Greek were written, γνωθι σεαυτον. They mean "know yourself."

In the last chapter we saw that potential in the workplace is found at the intersection of two fields or areas associated with making choices:

1. All the unused and unexplored possibilities and options available to us now and in the future.
2. The willingness and ability to take advantage of whatever possibilities we choose to select from this field.

Awareness is the first and most essential step to becoming the person that each of us can be in the world of work and anywhere else in our lives. It is the key to greater satisfaction, self-esteem and joy. For organizations, awareness is the power to avoid mistakes and seize opportunities. Being aware means being present mentally and knowing what is happening, what we are doing about it and why. Unawareness is the opposite: getting lost in concepts or daydreams and taking action without knowing why or considering what will result.

WITHOUT AWARENESS, we have no appreciation of the nature or extent of the options before us. We also have no knowledge of how to make wise judgments or what we need to turn potential benefits into reality.

Peter Drucker says: "Most people think they know what they are good at. They are usually wrong. More often, people know what they are not good at — and even then more people are wrong than right."[3] Being self-aware is one of the skills we need to use our gifts to enrich our lives and the lives of others. We must

---

[3] Drucker, Peter F., Managing Oneself. Harvard Business Review, 1999. (March-April): 65-74.

notice when old habits and assumptions block our path and hold us back. We must adapt continually to cope with whatever life brings us, both the good and the bad.

Our personal potential is a permanent part of us. It is not always obvious, but it is there just the same. If we want to find it, we have to look deeply within instead of skipping along on the surface of things, trusting in business as usual. We must become unrivalled experts in our own minds, emotions, behaviors and reactions. No one else can do this job. I am the only person who is around me 24 hours of every day. I am the only one who can be aware of each thought and feeling. Only I know all my concealed motives, hopes and dreams. No one else, however wise or expert, has full access to what is going on within me.

Potential as a process

Action reveals potential and changes it from an abstraction into something that produces real effects and consequences. Potential is a *process* not a thing. In the English language, potential is a noun. In reality, it is nearer to being a verb. When we limit our potential, we limit our *actions*, not just our concepts. If our processes are narrow and constricted, based on doing what we have always done and thinking what we have always thought, the actions we take will be similarly limited and ineffective.

The potential of organizations and teams is found primarily in the systems that they use. Team potential is not the mere sum of the potential of the team members. A team of highly talented people can be woefully ineffective if they fight continually or cannot agree on the action to be taken. Poor systems in an organization will prevent effective action regardless of the individual abilities and motivation of employees. Once again, potential is an active principle. When organizations become stuck in outdated habits, their responses to events are reactionary, limited and passive. The world changes, but they stay fixed in place: instead of leading they follow. In this situation, organizations must react to events and are no longer able to influence them.

Potential offers the key to greater satisfaction and achievement at work, but we will not recognize it without some idea of what we are looking for. Our goal is to understand the sources of potential, its causes and the effects it can have. Yet knowledge alone will not cause changes. Knowledge is a step on the way and an essential precursor to taking action. Without knowledge, we cannot make progress. We must understand how the process of realizing potential works, why each step matters and how our actions come together to produce results. We need a clear mental image to guide our search, so it is essential to devote time to looking within to see how our minds work. This is the starting point of our exploration.

Once we see clearly what needs to be done, and grasp why it matters, there is a natural urge to take action. Motivation is immediate and powerful. Action produces results which fuel experience. This is the essential cycle of learning: to understand what to do, to do it and then experience and reflect on the results. It is the only kind of learning that will lead to realizing potential. Book learning alone will not serve. We must take action and experience the causes and effects of the process for ourselves, so that we can understand how our teams, our organizations and we ourselves work, free from supposition, opinion and misinterpretation.

IMAGINE THAT you have never seen or tasted a banana. You do not know what a banana is. It could be a mechanical device, a small furry animal, or the name of the capital of a state in New Guinea. You have no idea.

A friend who knows about bananas tries to describe one to you. "It is a yellow fruit," she says. "It is about eight inches long and curved a little." Perhaps she shows you pictures, or tells you where bananas grow and how they are eaten. This is all useful information. By now, you will be able to recognize a banana. She also tries to describe the taste and assures you that you will love them, just as she does.

You are not convinced. What will a banana really taste like? You do not know if you will like the one she promises to bring for you tomorrow. Perhaps it will be disgusting and she will be disappointed — even a little hurt.

Your knowledge is extensive, but without personal experience it will remain incomplete. Despite all the knowledge you have gained, you have no idea whether you will enjoy eating a banana. The only way to find that out is to have the experience of putting one in your mouth and taking a bite. Even if you stop there, you will have gained two essential advantages you were lacking before.

- You know where to find bananas: in the grocery store, if you live outside the countries where they grow. You will not wander into the woods of New England, the swamps of Florida, or the moors of Scotland hoping to find a few bananas growing there.
- You know what to look for and how to recognize bananas in the fruit section of the store.

The search for our unused potential is exactly like this. We have to understand something of what potential is, just as our mythical friend with the deep ignorance of bananas has to know they are fruits, not roots or insects. We must know where to look for potential and where the search would produce frustration and a waste of time. And we need to have a mental picture of what it looks like, so we will recognize it when we find it.

Knowledge is essential to get us started, but we will never discover whether some aspect of potential can truly work for us until we have the experience: until we take action and try it. It is the same with the banana. We will not know whether we like bananas until we take a bite. All the parts of the process must take their proper places.

- We must begin by understanding as much as we can about potential, so we know where to look and how to recognize it.
- Then we set out to explore our organizations and our minds and hearts, looking in the right places to discover unused and hidden gifts.

✳ When we have found some untapped gifts, we have to take action and produce some result so we can experience it for ourselves and decide whether we like the taste.

It is not a process that others can undertake for us. We cannot rely on second-hand experiences and well-meaning advice. This is a journey that each of us must take for ourselves or never take at all.

Quick fixes do not work

Sometimes it is tempting to look outside to see if we can find some quick tips or shortcuts to help us: a recipe for success that we can follow to save ourselves a lot of time, trouble and false starts. I have an obstinate presumption that if a truly effective recipe for success existed, the book that contained it would be the only one still on sale. Bookshops have many shelves of books on the subject of self-development, each with its own numbered list of habits or steps to follow. The fact that there are so many of these books is, for me, the strongest evidence that none of them has the answer. They may be inspirational to read, but they do not seem to produce the goods over the long run.

It is natural to look at admirable people and wonder whether their good qualities might rub off on us if we behave as they do. We dream about our goals and quietly ignore our lack of plans to achieve them. The literature on role models and successful leaders makes good biographies, but will not supply road maps to success. We see these people like great architecture — completed works in all their glory, with no traces of the scaffolding and laborious processes that went into building them. All the false starts, mistakes, doubts or delays are invisible, except a few selected to display tenacity or willingness to overcome the odds. We have perfect hindsight into what made our role models admirable. The public likes simple answers to complicated questions, so everything gets reduced to formulas and numbered lists

Sadly, we are caught in a dilemma of time: we can only understand our world backwards from present to past; yet we must live our lives forwards, from present to future. Our grasp of what is going to work for us is always blurred by uncertainties about what lies ahead. We make plans and choose role models with hindsight and neglect to develop foresight. These role models lived in situations and contexts unique to them. Their times are gone and will never return. The same actions in today's context might turn out differently. The interaction of cause and effect that resulted in their success is more complex than most of us can grasp with any ease.

There are *no* quick fixes. Each of us is unique and lives in a unique context. What works for me may fail to deliver anything for you. The most we can do is try to be the finest version of ourselves that we can, given whatever events happen to help or hinder us.

Summary

* Life is uncertain. We cannot put ourselves in *absolute* control. That does not mean we are helpless. We can influence much of what happens around us.

- Awareness enables us to resume charge of our lives instead of letting habitual opinions, values and thoughts run things automatically. We get to make the decisions ourselves.
- To change the way something turns out, we need to understand the patterns influencing the outcome and what effect each one produces. The only sure way to change anything is to change what is causing it to be the way it is.
- We can step outside the fog of habitual thoughts and opinions, once we see them for what they are — just thinking. They are *not* the truth, even if we believe they are true. There is always more that we do not know and change that we do not expect.

FOUR

CONSCIOUS CHOICES

> Let us train our minds to desire what the situation demands.
>
> SENECA

> Don't confuse me with the facts when you can see I'm trying to make up my mind.
>
> ANONYMOUS

For most of our lives we make only occasional decisions that are truly conscious. Much of the time, we operate on automatic pilot. Instead of looking carefully and deeply to understand what is going on and what may be called for, we get a quick fix on things, automatically apply a response, and hurry on. Our culture, upbringing and habits provide these automatic decisions, along with opinions we have gathered along the way. In our rush to move to the next issue, we ignore the unique context for each event and deny ourselves the space to weigh all our options fully.

Organizations also operate mechanically. They let their systems take over while management is asleep at the wheel. Thinking becomes stale and repetitive. Fresh ideas rarely surface. Actions are mostly reactions based on simple rules of thumb or conventional wisdom. Managers are so driven to get short-term results that they ignore the obvious long-term implications of their decisions.

Some critics point out that people rarely use enough thought before taking action. Sometimes that is true. I see it differently. Most people do think, but their thinking is off target due to past conditioning and the systems within which they must operate.

When organizations operate in ways that are against their own best interests for long-term survival, there has to be something else that is claiming all their attention. Take managers obsessed with short-term results. The true reason for their limited horizon is their organization's systems. They are usually rewarded for reaching short-term goals. Their whole corporate culture typically demands this kind of action. It would take suicidal courage to do anything else. Even then, the chance of being allowed to continue on such a course would be minimal. These organizations act like teenage drug users: they sacrifice their future to immediate excitement and gratification, urged on by the pushers who make money out of their insane addiction — Wall Street, investment bankers and creative accountants.

Many of us have been brought up with inadequate ideas about what it means to think. Through years of formal education, we were taught to equate thinking with memory. We had to learn the answers from our teachers and use our memories to recall them for graded tests and examinations. Now, whenever we must think, we automatically start scanning our memories to see if we can find the right answer. If it is not there, we are lost. True thinking only *begins* when you realize you do not know the answer. You use your powers of thinking to work it out. The essential basis for all effective thinking is *not* knowing.

CONSCIOUS CHOICE unlocks unused potential because whenever we choose consciously, we open the possibility of reaching a new place. We can decide freely what is best. We are not tied to the past. When we act thoughtlessly, using the automatic responses provided by past habits, there is no possibility of change or growth. We may not like what happens to us, but we have left ourselves little option except to complain about other people or a malevolent fate. We have cut ourselves off from the ability to learn how we might change things for the better.

By making conscious choices, we put ourselves back into the driver's seat and switch off the automatic pilot. We know what we are doing and why we are doing it, so we can learn from the results whether they are favorable or not, and become more skillful next time. Conscious choice sets us free from repeating past mistakes. It releases us from the bondage of opinion and prejudice dressed up as fact.

WE HUMANS tend to confuse influence with control. We are all gamblers, secretly holding on to our lucky rabbit's foot while the dice are rolling; always trying to find ways to make things turn out as we want. If we are honest, we know we cannot control what happens in our lives, today or in the future. Control means being in charge and saying what will or will not be done. None of us has that power over events. Yet we are not powerless. What we do today makes a difference. It becomes part of the pattern of causes and effects that leads to the future. We cannot control events, but we can influence them.

The choices we made in the past have influenced where we are today. What we choose today will affect tomorrow. That is pretty much how the universe works and it is good news. We cannot change the past and we cannot control or foresee the future, but we *can* change the present. Since the present will influence what happens in our future, changing the present allows us to nudge the odds in our favor that things will play out to our advantage.

Whenever we make choices, those choices have consequences. This happens whether or not our choices are conscious. If we do what we always do, choosing habitually or automatically, we increase the odds that the future will most likely be a rough continuation of the past. If we make conscious choices, ones that are better aligned with the kind of person we aspire to be, the future will reflect that new present. It will not follow the past. How we choose to think and act today will determine, to a significant extent, how much of our potential we can realize in the future.

Cause and effect

Things do not just *happen*: they have causes. We might not be able to find the cause; there might be many causes that interact to produce what we experience. The causes may lie well outside anything we can influence or bring about, but there are always causes somewhere.

Let us set aside causes that have nothing to do with us or which arrive randomly. We can do nothing about them. We can also ignore most of the times when other people are the cause of events that affect us. They generally have little concern for *our* needs. They have their own agendas and act without reference to us. For building potential, what matters is to become aware of the causes over which we have some control — and the effects each one produces.

CAUSE AND EFFECT provides us with the basis for action. If we understand the cause, and can influence or change it in some way, we can alter the effect. If, for example, Sergio comes to understand that his habit of nit-picking and constantly pointing out other people's mistakes causes them to dislike and avoid him, he already knows what to do if he desires to be more popular. If Ellie grasps that what she intends as modesty appears to her boss as lack of initiative, she might be able to see why she does not get the promotion she knows she deserves.

Realizing potential results from using conscious choices as causes to bring about positive effects – for our careers, our colleagues, our business or ourselves. To do this, we have to explore the links between causes under our control and the effects they bring about.

This is not a simple process. Imagine a mass of basketballs being thrown onto a court by hundreds of different people. There is a prize for getting your ball to land in a specific place, so each person throwing tries to choose the track of the ball. They are thinking carefully where to throw it and what it will do when it lands. But there are so many balls — all bumping into one another and causing random deflections and collisions — that many of the intended throws turn into something quite different.

That is how life is. We throw our ball, but events make our intended throw turn out differently. It is no matter that this happens. If we are thoughtful and skillful, we can still produce the results we want a great deal of the time, which is better than throwing shots at random, or always in the same place, and trusting to luck. Winning part of the time is the best we can ever manage, so even a small increase in the number of times we succeed in our intentions will produce major benefits.

Awareness and conscious choice

Awareness and conscious choice are as closely intertwined as thorns in a briar patch. Without awareness of yourself and all the causes that arrive with you, no choice can be conscious. Causes go along with us like fleas on a stray dog. However much we scratch, we cannot get rid of our passengers. Ignoring them does not work either.

A SPARK FROM HEAVEN?

When someone asks me to make a decision, I bring all my prejudices, opinions, likes, dislikes, fears, hopes, antagonisms and knowledge along. I am not a single unite. I am a committee — a pretty bad tempered and cantankerous one.

Like all committees, my mind has some members who wield greater clout than others. They hog the floor and shout twice as loud as the next person. They get together and rig the committee elections so they will hold all the positions of power. And once they have a taste of power, like politicians the world over you will not part them from it.

Most committees — be it the Houses of Parliament, the US Congress or the board of directors of a major corporation — take good care to make sure that no one has more power than they do, at least where it matters. They make sure they are sovereign. The nominal people they serve, voters or shareholders, are only allowed to exercise vestigial rights of choice every few years. But our minds are more like medieval kingdoms or the Roman Empire. There is an absolute ruler who can always overturn the decisions of the senators — and even chop off a few heads to get attention. The trouble is, he or she is nearly always asleep.

The effect of improving our self-awareness is to keep our internal emperor awake and alert. Then we can see what is going on — what all the various habits and emotions and opinions on the committee are doing. Who is taking charge? Who is running our lives to their agenda, not ours? Since our internal emperor has supreme power if we decide to use it, we can intervene and overturn doubtful decisions. Of course the habits will fight back as much as they can. They have been used to running everything themselves and keeping the emperor asleep. They will suggest that all this watchfulness and attention is not necessary. It is so much bother, such hard work. Better relax and leave it to the professionals. Take no notice. If we want to affect how our lives run, we have to make sure *we* make all the important decisions.

Data, information and knowledge

Our automatic responses keep us unconscious and out of the loop by managing the information that we receive. They do exactly what any group of subordinates does to keep the boss out of their hair — they filter information and supply carefully crafted reports to make sure that the boss only has the knowledge that they approve. Here is how the process *ought* to work.

1. *Data* is collected, collated and organized, so that meaningful patterns and linkages can be seen. Random data is useless.
2. Correctly processed data becomes *information*. Now it can be sifted, explored and understood.
3. Information that is correctly understood becomes *knowledge*. It can be combined with other things we know and used to build an accurate picture of what is happening around us.
4. Knowledge is the basis for sound decisions and purposeful *action*. Action without knowledge is foolhardy. Knowledge that stops short of action is useless.

A SPARK FROM HEAVEN?

Our habits of mind act as powerful filters, continually sifting whatever data reaches us, letting this piece through, directing that piece to the garbage pile before it ever reaches our conscious mind. To be fair, it needs to be like this. So much raw data comes to us all the time that our brains would be completely unable to process it all.

For the moment, what matters is to see how we allow our habitual values, beliefs, attitudes and modes of thought to feed our conscious minds only what gets past their inspection. We form a view of the world, derived from these mental habits, and use it to determine what we can and cannot do, what is important and valuable and what is worthless. Self-awareness lets us identify our entrenched mental habits and identify what they are doing below the level of normal awareness. *We* have constructed this set of filters — or allowed our habits to build it. We can remove or bypass it whenever we want. Without awareness, we start to see our view of the world — our set of filters — as the only one there is. It becomes the unquestioned truth, fixed and absolute. Opinions become prejudices and values become rigid and fixed. Thoughts are treated as facts. We harden and solidify and lose our ability to grow and adapt. We start to expect the universe to fit *our* requirements. When it does not, we assume the right to feel aggrieved.

THERE IS an important distinction here. What we see, or know, or experience may well be true, but that does not make it *the truth*. The truth is absolute, fixed and unchangeable. It cannot be challenged. What we see to be merely true today, we may see as untrue tomorrow when some new information becomes available. Our knowledge — what we believe to be true — is always relative. It is true only in relation to what we know *now*. The truth is absolute. It is always true in every circumstance, regardless of what we know or do not know.

Groups, organizations and whole cultures become convinced that their view of things is the truth. They fight wars with anyone who disagrees. They punish heresy and banish or execute those who question. As quite a few innovators have discovered, large organizations are sometimes extremely unfriendly to those with ideas that do not fit the prevailing view of the truth. Look around and see how many people, who created new industries, new types of products and new ways of doing business, had to do so by setting up their own organizations. In many large, well-established businesses, creative questioning is about as welcome as a skunk in a perfumery.

Summary

* The more consciously we choose our actions, words and opinions, the more influence we will have over our lives at work and everywhere else.
* Knowing ourselves and acting on that knowledge are the basic steps in discovering and realizing our potential.
* Every choice is an opportunity to change. Every decision contains the possibility of altering the future. If we ignore these chances to influence

our lives, we must put up with whatever comes along.

✳ These four questions, if we answer them honestly and thoughtfully, will best prepare us for the journey towards our potential:
1. Do I already contribute everything at work that I know within myself that I could contribute?
2. What precisely is missing?
3. What is stopping me from making that extra contribution?
4. What am I doing that sabotages my own progress?

FIVE

STRENGTHS AND VALUES

> Throughout history, people had little need to know their strengths. A person was born into a position and line of work: the peasant's son would also be a peasant; the artisan's daughter, an artisan's wife, and so on. But now people have choices. We need to know our strengths in order to know where we belong.
> — PETER DRUCKER

> Genius means little more than the faculty of perceiving in an unhabitual way.
> — WILLIAM JAMES

Our personal potential lies within us — in our values, in the ways that we use our minds to grasp ideas and make decisions, and in how we choose to take action in the world. If we are willing to undertake this journey, we will find quickly that we have more potential than we ever realized and far more than we normally use. What is more, finding and using it will add greatly to our enjoyment of working life. Our potential is waiting to be let out. We only have to take the conscious decision to find and release it.

MOST OF US think we know what our potential looks like. It is virtually certain we are wrong. We do not understand our true strengths and weaknesses because we collect information about ourselves so ineffectively. We pick up bits and pieces with no coherent aim in mind. We jump to premature conclusions. We are highly selective: we only listen to good news when we are feeling good and focus on bad news when we are depressed. We almost never give ourselves enough time to discover how our actions have really turned out.

To provide a sound basis for development, strengths need staying power. They have to be capable of improving for years to come. What about the experience of starting an activity in a rush of enthusiasm, only to find the interest and energy gradually draining away? While we were performing, say, at the beginner's level, the effort was offset by some interest. Once the demands of progress increased, the activity was no longer sufficiently attractive to make it worthwhile. We found less motivation to stick with the learning curve. Our initial performance may have been good, but the activity held little potential for us beyond that point. Given a better sense of how we perform at work, we may see that what we do well today is not necessarily a *true* strength, at least in terms of our potential.

To construct a satisfying and successful career, or an organization that is a market leader, it is essential to know where potential lies. No one can produce good performance or a sound organization from weaknesses. Good work comes from using strengths and from nowhere else. The key to finding success and fulfillment is simple: discover our long-term strengths — our potential — and put ourselves where we can make best use of them and where they will be most valued. If that seems hard to achieve, it could be because we often make mistakes in understanding where potential can be found. That is why it is crucial to take time out to explore our potential in full: so we can get it right, make it clear to others, and start out in a direction we can stick with.

Watching ourselves

The simplest way to discover unused talents is to pay careful attention to ourselves over long periods and in many different contexts, noting thoughts, feelings and actions carefully *while they are current*. Reflecting after the event is better than not reflecting at all, but memory is fallible. Later thoughts will be tainted by justifications and rationalizations. Noting what we are doing while we are doing it opens up the possibility of change. We fill the container of potential slowly, drop by drop. It is a process which lasts a lifetime.

THREE STEPS are needed to discover and then make full use of our potential:
1. Exploration, in depth and without haste.
2. Patient removal of blockages.
3. Long-term, continuous development and learning.

The first step increases self-awareness and gets beyond superficial judgments about strengths and weaknesses. The second step aims to cure ignorance and arrogance. We must not jog along and let our automatic habits take the strain, or we will become narrow and parochial, priding ourselves on knowledge in some limited area and ignoring our ignorance of the rest of the world. If we look at ourselves dispassionately, and listen without judgment and defensiveness to what others say, we will see quickly what is in the way of progress. The third step involves working to broaden our minds and increase our options. Potential is always open, expansive and inclusive. Narrow opinions that disdain the wider context will never lead to potential. Usually they lead to foolishness.

Along the way, we should take careful note of habits that appear to block our progress or throw us off course. Blockages should not make us feel guilty or critical. We should note each blockage carefully and let it go. Drop it. Step past it and move on. We may have to do this a hundred, a thousand or a million times, but in the end the habit will go away for good. That will be a famous victory.

Do not waste time and effort on trying to deal with weaknesses that are not blockages to potential. Do not worry about areas where there is little strength on which to build. It takes great energy and determination to improve from completely awful to solidly mediocre; maybe three or four times — even ten times — what it would take to go from good to great.

Do we really want to work hard at becoming mediocre? Forget trying to be perfect in every way. It is impossible. Be the best possible version of yourself, even if that is not what you expected or the folks around you ordered. Anything else will condemn you to a lifetime of wasted effort.

How is more important than *what*

How we do our work is far more important than *what* we do. What we do — tasks, responsibilities and objectives — is specific to our present job and employer. A job with the same title and general duties in another department or firm will have many differences. *How* we do our work is personal and unique to us. We carry it with us wherever we go, transferring it to any new job or project. It is like a set of tools we take everywhere. As we learn, we add to the set and keep all the old tools polished and ready. Sometimes we discard a tool we know we will no longer need. As we become more and more skillful in using these tools we become more valuable.

Suppose someone discovers an intuitive skill with chisels. She could develop this to become a carpenter, a wood carver or a sculptor. Perhaps some person is never happier than when he has a wrench or spanner and a piece of machinery to work on. A natural feel for machines might enable him to become a top engineer. If you love the feel of a pen in your hand and paper in front of you, writing might be a good career direction. The point is to discover what works for you, then develop it as far as you can go, ignoring most everything else.

Potential is in the *how*, not in the *what*. It is the *how* that determines how well we do the *what*. It is the *how* that we can take to different fields of work, if our hearts propel us there. And as for satisfaction, the *what* may be the measure of success, but it is the *how* that got us there.

Organizations are much the same. They are tempted to follow fashion, just like individuals. They suffer from inflated egos and unrealistic choices. At some time, many extremely successful corporations have fallen into the trap of believing that success in the field they know, and were established to exploit, can be simply transferred to a totally different market. Typically, they embark on ill-conceived acquisitions or diversifications, often losing a great deal of money in the process. We would all do better to find what we do best and stick to that.

Kick-starting the process

Organizations and individuals can kick-start the activity of developing greater awareness by using a concentrated process of discovery and evaluation:

* Diagnostic procedures will help us think about ourselves in a systematic way, collecting our thoughts into useful categories and simplifying the search for important patterns.
* We can discuss openly what we have found. This often provides deeper insights and the encouragement to explore still further.
* We can spend time in introspection, asking powerful, probing questions and working with determination to uncover the answers.
* We can sharpen our observation of others, not to judge and criticize, but to provoke ourselves into considering whether we also behave as we see them behaving — and, if so, why.

We will always do our finest work by sticking to what suits us best; so once we have found what that is, we need to act on the knowledge. We have to *realize* our unused talents.

REALIZE has several meanings. It can mean to understand or grasp; it can mean to see something we have missed before; or it can mean to make conceptual things real and accessible to us whenever we need them. In working with potential, all these meanings are valuable. We understand our potential, see things that we have missed before and then bring what we find into the real world.

When we discover unused potential, it will most likely be undeveloped and raw. We may have the *potential* to become knowledgeable and skillful and experienced in that area, but right now we are almost completely incompetent. Lack of competence is always the *least serious* blockage to capability because it is the easiest to remedy. The *most serious* is unwillingness to pay sufficient attention for long enough to learn.

Our potential always begins with a lack of any significant competence. This has caused some people to get things wrong. Competence is the *aspiration*, the goal of our endeavors. It is where we will be, once we have completed the task of realizing our potential. We always begin learning any skilled task in a state of ignorance and inability to do it at all, let alone competently. To build competence we need a willingness to pay attention, some suitable ways to learn and develop, and the time and opportunity to use them. The objective of our efforts is not to change us into something else that other people will approve. Far better to seek out enjoyable work, do well and take good care to avoid anything that is not likely to produce better than mediocre or average performance. We are who we are. Attempts at radical change rarely succeed for long. *Our goal is to find out what we are likely to do best in the world of work and move steadily towards it, clearing any blockages out of our way.*

Where do we fit best?

Our potential is part of who we are; part of our unique variant on humanity. As an added bonus, it will improve our results and add to our enjoyment. Remember the last time you did something that you really felt was part of who you are? Remember how good it felt to express what you have inside you, openly and freely? That is what we are aiming to bring into our work: that sense of freedom, spaciousness and pleasure at doing what we have it within us to do, and doing it well.

These are the essential stages to the process of exploring and realizing individual or organizational potential:

* Motivation (willingness to pay sufficient attention and make the effort required).
* Recognition (seeing what matters and where we belong).
* Opportunity (taking the chances life offers and gaining support through increasing our credibility).
* Choice (taking action to make potential skills into real, demonstrable ones).

It is *essential* to ask two questions. First a question aimed at making the right choices about work and career: "What is the nature and extent of my potential?" Then the practical application: "Where do I belong?" Until we have answered the first question, the second is impossible to resolve.

To find potential, we need the motivation to start plus the determination to sustain our efforts and attention long enough to make a difference. Recognition comes next, based on exploring how we function today and how we *could* function in the future. After that, we need to take action in order to make our potential real. That means seeking out the opportunities we need and deliberately stepping beyond our familiar *comfort zones* and old, outworn habits.

DO NOT TRY to look too far ahead. We cannot plan our future with any certainty, especially if we try to look decades into the future. No one can tell what may come along. If we set our hearts on some specific outcome or event, we may become rigidly attached to it, and persist long after all hope of achieving it is past. When we know what we do best, and where we belong as a result, we will have a clear course to steer. Regardless of the shocks and buffeting in our lives, we can keep returning to that course. Potential only functions when we are flexible and open to unexpected possibilities, taking any opportunity that will lead us in the right direction and improvising freely to cope with all the unknowns. We must stay firmly focused on our goal — to realize as much of our potential as possible, given our circumstances — yet be extremely flexible about the means of achieving it.

Events *will* knock us off track. That is how life is. It is like trying to steer a ship in a storm. We know where we need to go, but the wind and tides keep swirling us around and pointing the bow in the wrong direction. Any chance we get, we have to get back on our course. We do not simply hold the wheel fixed rigidly in one direction. That is a recipe for meeting disaster on the rocks. We keep correcting the course and compensating as best we can for the effects of the storm. If we keep this up, firmly focused on the correct direction but constantly flexible about how to get back to it, we will come safely to harbor.

Summary

- The power of values lies in how they make us *feel* about an option, idea or even a person. Many decisions are emotional, fueled by values.
- Values and thought processes easily become automatic. When they do, their power is undiminished but we no longer notice them. In time, they control much of our lives, like a virus taking over a computer.
- We need to bring all our mental processes into consciousness, so we can see what is producing the way we think and behave, and what truly works for us.
- Potential is only present in actions and thought processes that match *all* of these criteria:
  - They are derived from our strengths.
  - They can be developed further.
  - They feel intuitively right.
  - They produce long-term motivation.
  - They facilitate learning.

SIX

MOTIVATIONS, EMOTIONS AND REASON

> Lord, grant that I may always desire more than I can accomplish
>
> MICHAELANGELO

> Let us not forget that the little emotions are the great captains of our lives and we obey them without realizing it.
>
> VINCENT VAN GOGH

It has been my experience that people nearly always have rational reasons for what they do. We may not agree with the reasons — or think they are rational from where we stand — but that does not change the situation. Even if the reasons have become so automatic that they are completely unconscious, they are always there. We will not change what we do (or think, or feel, or experience) unless we change the reasons that cause us to act (or think, or feel, or see) the way we do today.

The more effort or time something has taken, the stronger the reason behind it. This is an important piece of information. If strong reasons produce large effects, the bigger the change we want to make in how we spend our lives, the more passionate we need to become about it. Only the strongest of motivations will produce deliberately transforming effects. Of course, our lives may be completely turned upside down by some external event, like getting married or having a baby, but both of those usually require some passion along the way too.

WE WOULD all like to believe that our reasons for doing things are logical and eminently rational. Nice try. Deep down we know that we mostly do things from emotion. We feel good, so we act nicely towards people. We feel like a fight, so we pick on the mail delivery woman, or the checkout clerk, or the cat, or any other person we hope is not going to be able to fight back.

We generally do or say what feels right at the time — but may, sadly, feel silly later. Our emotions are much stronger than our rational thoughts. Remember when you last felt really angry, or frightened, or anxious? How well was your thinking working then? Were you coolly rational, taking a logical view of events and calculating the right things to do and say? Were you?

If you are anything like me, your mind felt like a mad jumble of incoherent thoughts, all of which kept circling back to the incident which provoked the fear, the anger or the worry. We make plans, only to drop them the next moment. Our imaginations go into overdrive, dreaming up ever more elaborate outcomes, whether we see ourselves triumphing over the evil folk who caused our distress, or suffering horrible shame and disgrace as our less appealing characteristics are shown to those around us. Mostly we keep going over the details of the problem, again and again, like a video playing an endless loop.

IT IS NOT very logical, is it? In any contest between our emotions and our thinking, there is usually the same winner. It does not have to be a turbulent situation. The much misunderstood phrase 'gut feel' is another way of describing situations where we do something because we *feel* it is the right thing to do, even if we cannot demonstrate that logically at the time.

What matters is to recognize that our emotions are fueled by our values, not by logical thought. We may use logic to justify what we value, but we will not give up our values easily, even if all the logical arguments in the world are marshaled against us.

The power of values lies in the way that they cause us to feel good or bad about an action, an idea, a person or a concept. It is our values that cause both guilt and elation. When we aspire to do the right thing, or act in the right way, our values are always there, telling us what is right. When our consciences trouble us in the early hours of the morning, they are doing so because we have somehow violated some of our values. Satisfaction, pleasure and joy are built on values fulfilled; guilt, remorse and shame follow whenever values have been ignored or abused.

Emotions always have their reasons. We tend to describe only thinking as rational, but that is not correct. If we use the word rational in the sense of coming about because of some reason, emotional decisions are just as rational as intellectual ones. The only difference lies in the type of reason: not reason based on logical thought, but reason based on *values*.

VALUES ARE deeply embedded in our being. They are the origin and location of our sense of who we are. Values tell us what is good, bad, right, wrong, important or not worth bothering about. They are so familiar and automatic that we rarely recognize it when they operate, but they can stop any thought, action or choice before it begins to register in our conscious minds. Because of this, values are probably the best place to start looking for potential. No amount of good advice or urging on by others will work if we do not feel within that we have this potential and — by heavens — we are going to bring it out and use it.

There is no inevitable alignment between values and strengths. Just because we do something well does not mean that it is truly important to us. It may get results and yet take our lives off track and away from where we belong. I know, for example, that I have some ability as a teacher. I also know that teaching is not right for me. I have tried it. I do it well enough for a while, but my heart is not in it and I soon begin to turn in a less and less satisfactory performance.

Once we have recognized our strengths, acting on them is rarely a problem. It is the natural thing to do. Acting on values may cause us more difficulty. It may be inconvenient, or unpleasant, or make us go against our friends. We may even have to stop doing some things we have learned to do rather well.

Matters of the heart

Values are matters of the *heart*. Our potential *always* aligns with what is in our hearts, even if our heads have learned to think differently. Going against your heart is a poor idea and the cause of much frustration, misery and depression. It drains all the pleasure and satisfaction out of life and produces hell and drudgery. It is rather easy to fill people's heads with ideas, opinions and notions. The media do it on a daily basis. We pick up all kinds of thoughts and statements, often with little care, and treat them as our own. Mostly we drop them just as easily. Ideas have power only when they seize our hearts as well as our heads. Our hearts are less easy to fool and less willing to pick up strange opinions from others. They are also less willing to drop what they have once accepted. Our hearts have the power to engage our emotions in a cause, be it good or bad. That is why it is such a serious matter when some fanatic or dictator manages to instill an evil purpose in the hearts of others.

OUR VALUES tell us what is good, bad, right, wrong, important or irrelevant. Although we rely on them totally, they do not always tell us the truth. As we have seen, others can hijack our values to serve their own ends. We can have mistaken thoughts and mistaken values. Terrorists destroy people and themselves because of the values they hold about their causes. Are they values that benefit the world? Hardly. Are they sensible? Not unless you think being a suicide bomber is sensible. Are they powerful? Powerful enough to kill.

This is how to spot a value that may be acting like a computer virus, determined to take over your life to serve its purpose. Potential is *always* open, expansive, inclusive and flexible. It sees possibilities in everything and is never dogmatic or punitive. Any value that seems to work in the opposite way should be suspect, if it is narrow, limiting, rigid and dogmatic; or if the value excludes people and sees only one right way — its own; or if it seems to be leading you towards some limited view of the possibilities in the world, take great care. It could well be a values virus.

MOST OF US have nice, workaday values. Many came from our families, who tried to bring us up to hold the values approved by society and the circles in which our parents moved. We have added more of our own, taking them from whatever seems to be useful and worthwhile — friends, good books, people we admire, our own experiences. Some we have proven through experience; others we have accepted as the entry requirements of the groups we belong to — from golf clubs and fraternities to churches or temples. We have even picked up some from the organizations who have employed us.

LIKE POTENTIAL itself, our values are not things. They are *processes* — processes of *valuing* or *evaluating* — fueled by emotions more than reason. Values work all the time, unconsciously and automatically. As soon as something comes to our attention, we evaluate it. Is it good or bad, pleasant or unpleasant? Do we like what we see, think, experience or imagine? Do we dislike it or fear it? Our values are constantly at work in our lives. Since my values are the standard by which I judge right and wrong, they have to be correct. And if I change them, the changes will be correct too — absolutely, unquestionably correct.

A SPARK FROM HEAVEN?

Whatever our values, we have a right to hold them freely so long as they do not involve antisocial activities like eating garlic in bed, murdering our neighbors, or mowing the grass at 7.30 a.m. on Sundays. In the pursuit of our potential, these two aspects of our values are especially important.

1. We believe our values are unquestionably right.
2. We are usually quite unaware of how much impact they have on what we think, say or do.

Values are, by definition, valuable and important to the person who holds them. They determine what he or she sees as right and wrong. So they are *right* — at least until others are taken up to displace them. At any specific time, the values we hold are completely right in our eyes. Which means that any opposing or different values must be wrong, equally without question.

We are so used to our own values and the values of the society in which we live that it is easy to assume they are the only ones — and even easier to assume they are the only right or *good* ones. That is why there is racial and cultural intolerance in the world. If our values are correct, anything else must be wrong. And our values are, by definition, always the right ones, whatever they are.

Unconscious values

Values have a tendency to become unconscious and automatic. Automatic values are still as powerful at raising emotions and controlling decisions, only now we no longer question or notice them. They are so much part of us. Like the pattern on the wallpaper in the guest room, we cannot recall exactly what they are with any clarity. They are just there: the unspoken and unexamined assumptions that rule our lives. When we need them, they are present in an instant. We need no effort to bring them into action. We have lived with them all our lives, more or less, and they are old friends whom we trust implicitly. When they become automatic, whole areas of our lives — and many opportunities — will be ignored without any conscious decision.

One way of spotting when we are operating from a powerful or *core* value that is becoming unconscious is to notice when some sense of righteousness creeps into our attitude. We may get a little pompous and priggish about what we know to be right, especially if it indicates that someone else is ignorant and astray. We begin to preach and patronize, going out of our way to set the other person straight. We become bores or prudes.

Our core values tell us what we should devote our lives to, so they are central to the motivation we need to find and access our potential. We also need to keep some sense of balance to get the best from core values in terms of passion and energy, without tipping over into the self-righteous zeal that convinces us that what we are doing is for other people's good, even though their screams are getting on our nerves.

Whenever our values become automatic and habitual, they govern our actions and start to close down conscious choice. The processes of judging, evaluating, or sorting the important from the irrelevant takes place with no input from our conscious minds. Unconscious habits are the most common blockages to potential; and ingrained, instinctive values — habits of evaluation with strong emotions built in — are the most powerful and tenacious. The only way to deal with them is to bring them out into the open and subject them to the antidote to all habits: conscious choice. We must do that even if it means questioning assumptions that we have previously used to underpin our whole lives.

Habitual thinking

How often are you aware of thinking? Now I have mentioned it you will be aware, but were you conscious of thinking a moment or so ago? Not aware of your thoughts — the *content* of your thinking — but of the *act* of thinking itself? We think all the time we are awake (and while we are asleep, if you count dreams), but we are rarely aware of the *process* of thinking. It just happens. Thoughts come and go, some pleasant, some not. We act on them or ignore them, or try to push them away, but they are so much a continuous part of our lives that we never notice the process of thinking, just as we do not notice our breathing until we get a cold and start to wheeze. We do not know how we are thinking, or how our values are affecting us, or where our emotions are coming into play. We do not know how our minds are functioning.

The way that we use our minds — the act of thinking itself — limits the information we will take in and controls how we will process it. Our brains constantly filter our perceptions, discarding most of what comes along as unworthy of conscious thought. It is either acted on automatically or discarded. Conscious thinking is the mind talking to itself, making sense of what it has taken in. If the major part of our mental activity takes place outside our consciousness, it will dictate what we can see, how we process any information we get, and how we take decisions.

HOW WE THINK also has a decisive effect on our behavior. It is not the only influence. Our emotions play a major role, as does our cultural inheritance and the ways others have taught us to behave. Because behavior is the only *visible* part of what is going on within, it gets most attention from those who want to influence what we do. There is a tendency to see it as something separate from the thoughts, emotions and values that bring it about. This is a mistake. In working with potential, we must be clear about what is influenced and what does the influencing: to distinguish correctly between cause and effect. Trying to improve performance from the outside (working with effects) is rarely successful. Understanding the patterns that lead to our behavior (working with causes) is far more effective. As we explore our potential, our behavior will change whether we want it to or not. We cannot develop fresh aspects of ourselves and remain the same.

Over time, our thought processes become as habitual and unconscious as our values. We are only aware of the contents of our thoughts, not the ways we handle them. To test this, ask yourself these questions:

* How are you thinking right now? Not what, *how?*
* Are you tightly focused on the detail of what you are reading? Are you just getting a general impression, skimming over parts that do not seize your attention?
* Are you thinking about what you are reading, or just trying to take it in?
* Do you like to put the book down from time to time and rehearse ideas in your mind? Do you mentally argue with the author?

* Do you prefer explanatory text, or illustrations and diagrams?
* Do you only really engage with stories and case studies?
* Is this typically how your mind works? Do you know? As you notice what you are doing, does it change?

THE ROUTE to potential is through learning, and how we think has a major impact on how we learn. Realizing potential demands we use the method of learning that is best for us. Reflecting on the processes we use habitually when we are thinking takes effort. It is not a normal activity to wonder just how we do it, like the centipede that tried to recall which leg he stepped out on first and lay helpless in the path, unable to remember how to walk. Are we aware, truly aware, that other people use quite different processes? Is that perhaps why we sometimes find they do not easily understand what we are trying to tell them? Whenever we let unconscious, habitual thought processes and values take charge of our minds, much of our potential will be hidden or blocked. We can no longer discover fresh ways to think that could reveal more of our potential. We will be left with the nagging feeling that our lives have been less than they might have been.

I will devote much more space later to habits of thinking. For the moment, let us concentrate on how thought processes figure in the search for potential.

Paths to learning

Suppose I learn best by arguing things through with others. If I try to sit at a table and learn by reading on my own, I may find learning next to impossible. I will get bored and fidget. I will find excuses to do something else. I will not be able to recall what I have read and will become frustrated and demotivated. But if I learn best by considering all the details, carefully and in depth, solitude to read and reflect may be my best friend in finding my potential. I can check back on what I have read, verify the details and quietly get everything straight in my mind.

Most educational institutions are organized around a single way of learning applied to everyone. This makes for administrative ease and conformity of teaching requirements. Whether the chosen approach is learning by rote or by discovery, it is still a one-size-fits-all approach. That is why some able and imaginative people perform so badly in school, only showing their true ability later in life. Since no one — including ourselves — stops to find out what learning process will suit us best, we see what is on offer as all there is. As a result, we will grow up with another set of habitual mental approaches that serve us badly in our quest to fulfill our potential.

A key part of any exploration of potential must be to find out what mental habits have been formed, then consider whether they are useful or produce a blockage. We may be going against the grain of our nature in order to stick with an approach that has rarely given either satisfaction or success. How else might we think and learn? What are the options?

One good place to look for clues to our natural mental processes is to explore what our minds do when they are off duty: when we are relaxing, pursuing a hobby, or enjoying ourselves with things we believe do not matter so much.

Suppose I spend my working days in drudgery, writing reports that are constantly returned for revision, but spend my evenings in passionate debate with friends over something trivial, like the best route to Philadelphia. Maybe I naturally think better when talking than writing. Some people think best by sketching ideas on paper. The sketch can be crude and indecipherable. It does not matter. It is the process that matters. I often think best by ranting: expounding my ideas at length and with deep conviction to my wife — who has developed highly selective listening and the patience of a saint. I have lost count of the times when I pause, mid-sentence, to rush for some paper to capture an idea that only surfaced as I was trying to explain the old one. Walking fast and talking to myself works well too, but earns me a reputation for eccentricity and causes passers-by to laugh.

Summary

* Most of us have only sketchy ideas about our potential. To find it, we need to begin with a stronger sense of how we operate best.
* Good work comes from finding where we belong and can use our strengths to the fullest extent. That is true for teams and organizations, not just individuals.
* Weaknesses should take up the minimum possible time and energy. They should be ignored or avoided where possible, and only ever worked on until they are no longer such barriers to progress.

SEVEN

FAITH IN THE JOURNEY

> Faith is the substance of things hoped for, the evidence of things not seen.
> — ST. PAUL

> Faith is an excitement and an enthusiasm: it is a condition of intellectual magnificence to which we must cling as to a treasure and not squander.
> — GEORGE SAND

In the last chapter, we considered where to look for potential. Our goal is to find where individuals, teams and organizations will fit best into their respective worlds. That is the only spot that will open satisfying and productive options and possibilities.

Just as in the tale of the lost motorist who asks a local how to reach his destination, our response to this journey may be, "If that is where you say you are going, I wouldn't start from here." Still, we are where we are and there is nowhere better to start. We have already built up some idea of potential and begun to understand something of the experiences along the way. What we need now is a map to guide us and the faith to trust it. Maps have many purposes. One of the least understood is their capacity to bolster faith in the journey and the capacity to complete it.

We already have some useful features to include on our map. We know that potential must be based on natural strengths. We know it must align with core values. It must be something we can believe in fully: a path to engage emotions as well as our intellect. It must point to a place in the world of work where we can truly belong.

Perhaps as we look around in our lives there seems to be little that fits such a lofty set of ideals. Many people's working lives are mostly dull and ordinary. Such people may aspire to fulfill their potential, yet lack the courage and confidence to take effective action.

The importance of faith

When I was a child, the roads in England were much as they had been for several centuries — only surfaced with tarmac. No motorways had been built. No M1 or M25 to promise fast travel but supply endless bottlenecks. Even main roads wandered between towns and villages, just as they had when stagecoaches or medieval pilgrims used them. Any long journey was an adventure.

The evening before we needed to make such a journey, my father would sit at the dining table with maps spread around him. Using a series of blank postcards, he would write down the towns and landmarks we would pass the next day, putting them in the correct order. In the morning, he clipped the stack of postcards to the dash of the car, so he could see at a glance which landmark or town to head towards next. We children could also follow the journey, eagerly looking for the next spot on the list. Sometimes it even kept us quiet for a few miles.

My father's directions gave us faith in our journey. As long as the towns and other landmarks arrived in the correct sequence, we were on the right road. The way might seem long and uncertain, but we knew we would make it in the end.

FAITH IS an essential ingredient in any process to realize potential: faith in ourselves and in the gifts we bring to the organization. Without faith, the normal setbacks and difficulties of life will overwhelm us. When other people bolster our faith in ourselves, they do us a greater service than they can imagine.

Many people and organizations never set out on the journey towards their potential because they lack any faith or confidence in the process. They doubt the possibility of a better future. They question their ability to do better, becoming cynical about development and skeptical of learning. In time, such doubts and fears turn into chains holding us in mind-numbing, dreary jobs that use barely a fraction of our true potential. Without faith, a working life is barely worth living.

Yet faith alone is not enough. We also need the facts: the real facts, not those we like or want to be true. The motivation needed to propel us towards our potential is based on a tricky combination: seeing ourselves as we truly are (and our world as it really is), while holding to an unwavering faith that we can get where we want to be. The leadership guru Jim Collins found just this blend of resolve and reality in top leaders who propelled their companies from good performance to greatness.[4] But it is not confined to such exalted ranks. You will find it in every successful person.

We must have the facts or our map will be based on false information. One of the characteristic behaviors I have found in many frustrated and disappointed people is a high degree of blindness to reality. They base their feelings and actions on an idea or concept, not on reality. That idea may be a negative one (the world is a nasty place and nothing I can do will ever change my misery); or an overly optimistic one (the world really is as I would like it to be and I'll ignore anything and anyone that suggests it is not). Either way, their actions and beliefs are based on false information. The results are suffering, frustration and lack of success. Reality is what it is. It will not change to something else because we want it to.

EVEN ABLE and successful people can find that their view of the world is so far adrift from reality that it blocks their progress. Leadership expert Chris Argyris found that many highly intelligent professionals had developed a kind of immediate defensiveness towards bad news that stopped them learning from their own mistakes.[5] They had little experience of failure and feared it deeply. Rather than take the risk of discovering that they might be wrong, they covered their eyes and avoided testing the facts.

We need to see events and ourselves as they are in reality, neither ignoring the bad parts nor being falsely humble

---

[4] See Select Bibliography under Chris Argyris, 1991.
[5] See Select Bibliography under Jim Collins, 2001.

about the good ones. Such realistic information places our faith on a sure footing.

Going it alone

My father drove tens of thousands of miles every year. He never relied on directions from other people. He always worked out his own route. This taught me something about going it alone, not just on physical journeys but in the journey of life as well. People can be essential to encourage and support us, yet we generally have to find our own way.

I am not belittling the support we can get from others, nor am I suggesting that we need to be so self-reliant that we scorn assistance or advice. We need friends and family to cheer us up when we feel down; to bolster our confidence; and to offer practical help and support. Yet we are the only ones accountable for how we live. Wise friends and mentors can jolt us out of complacency and give us the confidence to make things happen. They cannot do the work on our behalf and hand us the results. Fulfilling our potential is an active process. No one ever fulfilled their potential by waiting passively for someone to bring it on a plate. We must take action. We cannot expect others to find our potential for us. No one can know us that intimately. No one else can feel what we feel inside, or sense what we sense when opportunity sends a thrill of excitement through our minds. Nobody has a similar interest in our future happiness or success. When we rely on others to point us towards our potential, we become dependent on *their* knowledge and insight about the process. Some may prove to be reliable guides. Others will not.

A SPARK FROM HEAVEN?

IMAGINE walking through a city where you have never been before, trying to find a particular store. You have no map or directions and so must rely on asking passers-by to send you the right way. Unfortunately, everyone has different ideas about where the store is and how to get there. One person offers you a great short cut that is so complicated that you get lost after the fourth turn. The next person sends you in the opposite direction. The next contradicts that and sends you back again. "It is on the left, just a couple of blocks ahead," says another, full of confidence. After six blocks you are still lost.

That is what it can be like when we rely on various patent ideas and "infallible" directions to become successful in the world of work. People have their own agendas. Their directions are based on their interests not ours. They tell us what *they* would do, only we are not like them and what works for them is poison for us. Many offer to sell us a map, though these maps are not accurate; and some are designed mostly to send us where people are waiting to sell us still more things. There are plenty of people looking to involve us in their schemes. A few may even try to send us along dark alleys where their friends can rob us.

FORTUNATELY, none of us need to buy maps from other people. We each have our own, made of insights and experience derived from what we have noticed in the past about our strengths, our values and the opportunities that best fit who we are. Organizations have maps like this as well. Theirs are based on the knowledge of experienced employees and the systems that have stood the test of time.

A SPARK FROM HEAVEN?

By going through the exploration phase of discovering unused potential, we add information to the map: data on strengths that have never been fully exploited; information about the deepest values that have most effect on behavior; and the left-over habits that confuse and block the path. The better and more up-to-date the information in our internal map, the better it will serve to guide us. Poor internal maps tend to be full of hearsay, speculation and second-hand opinions.

When I was a teenager, I went to school in an ancient town in England dominated by a huge cathedral. In one corner of the cathedral hung the oldest surviving map of the world. Now it is in a special museum behind bullet-proof glass and you have to pay to see it, but in those days it hung on the wall in a simple case and no one thought much about it. The monk who drew it put Jerusalem at the center, of course, and his knowledge did not stretch to exotic places like Australia or Kansas, but we used to amuse ourselves trying to find countries or cities we recognized.

The edges of the map were special fun. The poor old monk had no idea what might be there. He had probably never been more than a dozen miles away from the place where he was born. So he filled in the spaces by using his imagination. There were huge birds, animals with five rows of teeth and men with no heads and eyes in their shoulders. Our special favorite was the guy with a single huge foot who lay on his back, using his foot as a sunshade. When imagination ran out, the monk turned to his last resort. In the blank spaces he wrote: "Here be dragons."

For many of us, the spaces outside our habitual comfort zones feel equally unknown and scary. Like the monk, we fill them with imaginary dragons. The monk's map was not useful for travel in his day. It would be laughable today. It lacks up-to-date information and accurate data. So do many of our internal maps. Happily, we can update them.

Summary

* Faith is an essential ingredient in potential: faith in ourselves, our ability to realize our potential and the gifts we can bring to our working lives.
* Cynicism and skepticism can prevent us even beginning the journey to discover our potential.
* Faith needs to be based on reality. For that we need to have the facts about where we are going and how to get there. We need a map. Fortunately, we all have one built-in.

EIGHT

POSTCARDS

> In traveling, a man must carry knowledge with him if he is to bring back knowledge.
>
> SAMUEL JOHNSON

> Compared to what we ought to be, we are only half awake. We are making use of only a small part of our physical and mental resources. Stating the thing broadly, the human individual thus lives far within his limits. He possesses power of various sorts which he habitually fails to use.
>
> WILLIAM JAMES

There are a small number of key indicators that point to true or genuine potential. I like to think of them as postcards, like the ones my father used to assemble before a long journey. They start with questions to help us choose the best route towards our potential; then change to queries that will tell us whether we are heading in the right direction. The last two will indicate when we have arrived. They are written for personal use, but require little change to be just as helpful to teams or organizations.

Does it align with our core values?

True potential always aligns with core values. If it does not — if it is something we think we ought to do or have been told would be good for us — we will never develop enough motivation to bring it to realization.

Thinking is not the same for everyone and nor are values. Your values will not be the same as mine. Mine are different than my sister's or my daughter's. Men's values tend to be different than women's values; though each individual's values are at least as likely to be different again. An American's values may well differ from those of a European or an African. Values are like fingerprints: a mark of our uniqueness, with the important difference that we get to choose at least some of our values and certainly to decide to change them any time we like.

It is important to act on the understanding that all values are relative. Describing something as relative is often assumed to belittle it. Only absolutes are seen as desirable. Yet an absolute value — even if such a thing existed — would be a dreadful tyrant, rigidly demanding complete subservience whatever the circumstances. We have laws that maybe come close to this on occasion, often prompting much anguish while producing little that could be described as justice. The context *always* changes the event.

For example, we all agree that stealing is wrong. The person who robs a bank, or cheats investors out of their savings, is punished for theft. What about the person who makes personal telephone calls at their employer's expense? Or uses company computer equipment for private purposes? Or takes stationery items from the company stock cupboard for personal use? Are these examples of theft? All involve taking something that does not belong to us and doing so without permission. If theft is an *absolute* term, they must be included. But many people might say they are not examples of theft — at least as long as the usages are minor. They change the context of the event by using words like "customary perks of the job" and stressing that the monetary amounts involved are small. That changed context makes theft a *relative* term.

MY VALUES are right — and so are yours, even if they are different. Right for you, that is: right in your perception, just as my values are right for me, given my experience and background. That is what relativity in values means. What is right for you in your context does not have to be imposed on me in mine. Of course, in my perception, your values may be wrong and I may become righteous about setting you straight. In a free society we rightly resist attempts to impose one person's sense of rightness on everyone else; yet our core values tempt us continually to overstep this boundary.

Suppose Angela has *achievement* as a core value. She feels passionately about the importance of setting goals and meeting or beating them. She judges much of her own value by the extent of her achievements. She values others in the same way.

Our potential is always found in the things we *have not* done yet, or in the options and possibilities we *have not* chosen. It is always different than our habits in some way. If it were not, it would be actual behavior — more of what we do already — not potential. But if Angela is passionate about achievement, any options that *do not* involve some degree of achievement will feel wrong to her. Not only will they feel mistaken, they will *be* wrong by her standards. Unless her core values change, she will not follow these options. Even if someone else pointed out all their benefits, the options are not aligned with her core values and she will not go there willingly.

Suppose Angela starts to think about her actions and choices and notices that she gets quite a kick out of the occasional party with friends. Perhaps she does not go too often, because she is busy achieving and taking time off for a party seems frivolous. But when she does go, she ends the evening excited and energized. This might indicate that she has an unacknowledged value based on building enjoyable, lasting relationships. She has not paid much attention to that part of her life — because there is an endless list of things to achieve — but it certainly does not *clash* with the core value of achievement. In fact, it aligns well, since creating a strong relationship is certainly an achievement worth celebrating. If she adds the skills of building relatedness to her skills of achieving results, the outcome could be both powerful (achievement) and companionable (relatedness). Those strong relationships are likely to assist her to achieve still greater results. They are aligned.

IN THE WORLD of values, you **can** have your cake and eat it. You can retain and build on your core values and continue to add new ones that express unused parts of your potential. The resulting mixture often makes the original core values more effective.

Here is another example, again using a core value for achievement. Strong achievement values often lead to constant competition, where achievement is judged by personal eminence. Only one person can come first. If achievement drive is not tempered and balanced by something like a value for relatedness, it can become so competitive that it ends up being unpleasant, even downright nasty. The person stills values achievement, but now it leads them to display domineering attitudes, aggressive behavior and critical condemnation rather than approval. We may applaud aggressive behavior on the sports field or battlefield, but few organizations can function if people within them spend much of their energy competing with one another.

Does it feel exciting?

Potential *is* exciting. It is fun. It is doing what comes most easily and naturally to us. After some time spent exercising our potential, we have greater energy, not less.

I do not mean that no effort is involved. It can be tough to realize some piece of outstanding potential. But it will not *feel* like hard work — at least, not in the sense of needing stubborn determination to overcome a constant wish to give up. Performers, from musicians through dancers to sports stars, have described a state known as *flow*, where effort is effortless and they know that nothing can go wrong .

When we connect with our true potential, we sense the excitement of *flow*. The expansive nature of potential lifts us to a state where possibilities are all around and choices become nearly infinite.

We may lack competence in the new area — in fact, we almost certainly will. We may be nervous and uncertain, yet through it all we will sense that thrill of excitement that arises when we know that something is truly right for us. It is bound to be exciting, just as looking out over the vastness of the ocean is exciting. It may also feel daunting. That is natural. We have so much more potential and so many more options than we usually allow ourselves to see. Like the ocean, the range of possibilities is vast. All we usually do is stay as close to shore as possible — perhaps even tied up in harbor — so the idea of setting sail into that vastness may be intimidating. But who has not thrilled to the idea of sailing to discover new lands? It is no longer possible in this physical world, but we can all be Magellan or Christopher Columbus in the worlds of our minds.

Does it build on our strengths?

Nobody can build a house without materials. A strong house, able to withstand life's constant assaults, needs tough construction. Imagine you have to build a tower that will reach into the sky and withstand hurricanes and tornados, but all you have for building material is a pile of old plywood and some cracked and crumbling secondhand bricks. That is what it is like for us if we try to build potential out of weaknesses. The raw material is not strong enough for the task.

Organizations have become fixated on what does not work instead of what does. They draw up models for excellence, but concentrate on the behaviors that fall furthest from the ideal. These organizations are constantly urging employees to correct their faults and bridge the gaps between the ideal and reality. Strengths are ignored in the drive to correct weaknesses. It is assumed strengths need no attention to go on functioning. This is nonsense. A neglected strength, like a neglected muscle or a neglected piece of machinery, soon works poorly, becoming weaker and more prone to problems. In time, the strength becomes another weakness.

Our natural areas of strength are the only sound basis for realizing potential. We cannot jump instantly from bungling beginner to assured expert. Developing ourselves needs time and persistence.

We may have systematically ignored at least some of our strengths at other people's bidding. We have an inner pull towards an activity, but suppress it because we are told it is useless or bad. As parents, we all bear some share of responsibility for suppressing things that our children find natural and easy, in the cause of making them fit into our notions of the right thing to do for a successful life. In our anxious care for their future, we risk trying to make them become what *we* wish, not what they have within them. Successful parents draw out their children's natural potential, even if it is for something the parents find incomprehensible. Successful leaders discover what their subordinates do best and use them for nothing else.

Recognizing natural strengths is not arduous. Natural strengths are all those things that we keep feeling drawn towards, even if we have been asked to believe that they are useless, disruptive, pointless or worthless. We should trust our intuition. We are continually drawn back to them because they are part of who we are.

Is this a stretch?

Anything within our comfort zone is *competence*, not potential. Competence means doing what we do already, only better. Potential is doing something new or extra: something that will stretch us and extend the breadth and range of our capabilities. Realizing potential always means stretching. If it is not something that goes beyond our habits, requiring us to step outside our comfort zone, it is not potential.

As Peter Block, author and consultant to governments and businesses, points out, we often ask ourselves too quickly how we are going to do something. By doing this, we focus on the difficulties instead of the possibilities.[6] We undermine our confidence in the goal and convince ourselves that we will be unable to achieve what we have set out to do. As we rush into how we will carry out our intentions, we lose the passion and motivation that inspired us in the first place; our habits and fears crowd around, each pointing to some new difficulty.

Another common aspect of deficit thinking is always to look first at what is missing or not working. Instead of the natural pleasure we could take in exercising our minds and skills to reach out towards something new, we become frozen by anxiety and fear of failure. All our attention is focused on the problems. Since attention causes objects to increase in power, these problems loom so large that we are defeated before we begin.

When I was a student at university, our Director of Studies had the infuriating habit of gathering as all together on the first day of the new academic year to tell us,

---

[6] See Select Bibliography under Peter Block, 2002.

in great detail, the complete program of work ahead. I never failed to leave those meetings feeling miserable and dejected. All that work! It seemed impossible to achieve without working twenty-four hours a day. But when I looked back at the end of the year, I would see that I had done everything he set out, plus many other things, and still had time for relaxation and an active social life. It was simply the mental effect of looking at everything at once and an involuntary habit of trying to work out immediately how I'd reach the goals set.

STRETCHING ourselves creates *more* energy than it uses. Remember what it is like to reach the end of a day or a week in which you have done little but routine work? How do you feel? I always feel exhausted and debilitated. Engaging in work that does not stretch or challenge us drains our energy.

Of course, if we push ourselves too far or too fast, we will also end up exhausted. People with high ambition run the risk of burnout, driving themselves so hard that their mental and physical resources cannot stand the strain. Trying too hard and pushing too far results in lowered capability and poor performance. Too little practice — and complacency with current achievements — also limits accomplishment. We have to reach a balance: enough stretch to keep us vibrant, alive and pushing our limits, without tipping over into strain and stress. This is where a good diagnostic and a coach can be invaluable, helping us to explore our limits and see the boundaries *before* we cause ourselves harm and stress. Once we have sustained an injury, the damage has been done.

Is it increasing our learning?

If no learning is involved, it is not potential. Learning is an essential part of the process of realizing potential, so the absence of any need for learning is a giveaway that this — whatever it is — is not part of potential. Whenever we repeat our past, we forego a chance to develop and learn. Although repetition can sometimes be a good way of increasing ease and facility, life is not like practicing scales on the piano.

To fulfill our potential we need the opportunity to learn: not just classroom learning — though this helps — but the chance to experiment with new ideas, accept wider responsibilities and gain fresh experiences. All higher animals play, both as young and (when they can) as adults. It is part of a natural process that expands and stimulates our minds. It also points to another aspect of what is needed for learning to be effective — security and confidence. It is tough to play or learn if you are afraid.

Repetition may make us more skillful in physical, recurring tasks, but it will not help us do anything *new*. We cannot connect with potential until we go beyond what we already know. When we repeat ourselves, we stay within our comfort zone where there is no potential. There was once, but we have already accessed it and turned it from potential into developed competence. Maybe it is already on the path to becoming habit. That is what happens to potential. Once we have accessed it and made it our own, we get used to it. It becomes habitual and habits, as we know, are the worst enemy of development.

Are we learning something, not <u>about</u> something?

The English language often uses the same word to mean two separate ideas, in this case learning *something* and learning *about* something. It is essential not to confuse the two kinds of learning. Learning *about* something means adding to the knowledge we have already. It is going deeper into what we already know. Learning *something* is discovering it for the first time, adding to our knowledge. Learning *something* — unlike learning *about* something — requires new events and new outcomes. The route to finding and realizing potential is through the kind of learning that broadens and adds to understanding. We can only learn in that way by trying fresh things. The more we repeat past behavior, the *less* we learn. Learning *about* something increases competence. Learning *something* new broadens and enhances potential.

The main difference between successful and unsuccessful people is the extent to which the successful ones consciously and continually engage in *learning something*. We have muddled it up over the years with partial ideas like intelligence quotients, personality traits or — Heaven forgive us — being made of "the right stuff." We have confused ourselves with assumptions about cultural differences, educational standing and racial stereotypes. Of course there are differences between people. Some do well and others poorly. *The ones who do well have developed more conscious access to their potential than the others.*

In all walks of life, people put into extraordinary circumstances — in wartime, for example — do amazing things that they did not believe they could do. Nothing had ever called for them to behave that way, but when the time came they did what was needed. Most were perfectly ordinary people, who accessed potential they did not know they had. They had not attended courses in personal transformation. They had not trained for the near impossible demands the world suddenly thrust towards them. Where did the ability to step up to life's demands come from? There is only one place it could have been — right there within them. When was it there? Whenever they needed it.

Does it broaden minds and open perspectives?

Potential is *always* expansive. It opens up our minds to new, wider viewpoints. It allows us to see farther. It brings things into our lives that make them fuller and more inclusive.

Many of us feel victims of today's working environment. There is so much detail and complexity: so much to keep track of and hold in our minds. Perhaps that is why we have a habitually short-term perspective, looking for quick results on every issue. Sales people are expected to develop *elevator pitches* to describe their product or service in 30 seconds or less. We are exhorted to "keep it simple, stupid." Top executives want all the options and arguments on complex issues set out on a single piece of paper. The media assume that our attention span, even on matters of great importance, must be measured in *sound bites*.

This relentless demand for speed and simplicity is counter-productive. Important issues cannot be reduced to a couple of paragraphs without serious distortion. Recent events on the stock market have shown that pressure for short-term profits easily leads to long-term failure and even fraud. If we give ourselves no time to stand back and reflect carefully about important judgments, we risk rushing headlong into avoidable disasters. We no longer see the forest for the trees. Sometimes, we cannot even see the trees.

Standing back to look behind the complexity to the underlying structures and patterns is an essential skill. The human brain does not deal well with too much information. It becomes confused and overloaded. But it can see patterns and assess their implications in ways that are far beyond the capabilities of the most advanced supercomputer. Nature produces its most complex creations from a small number of organizing elements. The universe is built from a handful of elementary particles and interactive forces. Business issues are no different.

We have too much information most of the time, not too little. Instead of arbitrarily pruning our perspective to fit a limited time and attention span, we should widen it to grasp the principles that lie behind it.

How we present issues to our minds is vital to how well they can respond. We confuse ourselves by trying to grasp all the details instead of looking for these organizing principles. We try to slice our experience into manageable pieces, so that we can control it. We isolate issues and categorize them: this is a marketing problem, that is a computer problem. Yet events come to us as a whole, not dissected into bite-sized pieces. By isolating them, we lose the context that allows us to make sense of them and see their importance. It is no wonder that people often spend weeks of effort on problems that have little or no relevance to anything of importance. Without a context, these people cannot realize how their priorities have become warped.

The natural expansiveness of potential lets us stand back and see the difference between *convergent* issues (where options must be narrowed down to a single, correct choice) and *divergent* issues (where there is no right answer and analysis cannot produce one). Finding the shortest route by road from New York to Los Angeles is a convergent problem: there is a right answer that can be reached by analysis of the information. Deciding where your business fits best into its industry and markets is a divergent problem. It is a matter of choice and judgment. There is no single, correct answer; indeed, there may be many equally coherent answers to the same question.

Does it produce more value, confidence or joy?

In many ways, this is the most important question of all. Potential makes us *more* of just about everything — more valuable to others, more confident in our ability and more courageous, joyful and successful. If something fails this test, the others scarcely matter. It will not be part of our potential. Realizing potential is always exhilarating. If it is not increasing our value, confidence and ability to have fun, it is not potential.

Can you imagine anyone at the point of death saying this to his grieving friends and relatives: "I've had a full life, full of efficiency, competence, task orientation and cost control. I've achieved my performance objectives and met my budgets. I've been a team player and always remembered to keep it simple"? Contentment arises from within us, not from outside. All of us have the potential to build lives that are rich with meaning and humanity.

Even within today's organizations, it is becoming clear that achieving a machine-like state of efficiency is neither good for business nor profits. As well as the power of ideas, you need the power of connection to people. People who love their work, love to learn, love to meet others and love to share and create the most value. People in organizations make choices about whom to trust and who merits their time and attention. They choose people whom they like and who treat them well: people who are fun to be around. When was the last time you willingly gave business, information or support to someone who is unpleasant, negative and a misery to be near?

Summary

* These are the key indicators of potential:
    1. Does this align with our values?
    2. Does it feel exciting?
    3. Does this build on our strengths?
    4. Can we feel this stretching us?
    5. Is this increasing our learning?
    6. Are we learning something, not just learning about something?
    7. Has our perspective been expanded?
    8. Do we now have more value, self-confidence and joy?

NINE

BLOCKAGES AND ANTIDOTES

> It ain't what a man don't know that hurts him; it is what he knows that just ain't so.
>
> — Frank Hubbard

> Human nature is not a machine to be built after a model, and set to do exactly the work prescribed for it, but a tree, which requires to grow and develop itself on all sides, according to the tendency of the inward forces which make it a living thing.
>
> — John Stuart Mill

One useful way of looking at performance is to see it as the part of our potential that gets through the interference we create in our lives. Timothy Gallwey, author of *The Inner Game of Tennis*, sees performance as a constant tug-of-war between our potential and our capacity to get in our own way.[7] Our thinking mind is always interfering, trying to control what is going on. As a result, we distort our natural responsiveness and skill, and so lessen our own performance. Have you noticed how often we say one thing but do another? Thinking usually shows itself in action at some stage, so we must have a reason for this apparently inconsistent behavior.

IT IS MOSTLY a matter of which thoughts are most powerful at the time: our conscious thoughts or the unconscious ones that usually run our lives. Our most powerful thoughts and feelings are the ones revealed in our behavior, so if we look deeply, we will find that what we do is always exactly in line with what the most influential elements in our minds at that time are telling us. Our conscious minds may propose one thing, but our powerful unconscious, automatic and habitual beliefs make sure we do something different.

The more care we take to explore our minds and our natural gifts, the more we will discover the unconscious ways in which we frustrate our own ability. One of the simplest ways to realize potential is to stop blocking the expression of our potential through unskillful actions and thoughts.

Suppose I decide consciously to try to look good to my boss. I volunteer to take on extra work, perhaps leading an important project. At the time, I fully intend to shine and earn golden opinions all around. However, once the work stretches ahead of me, my habitual sense of low self-esteem reasserts itself. I curse myself for having taken on

---

[7] See Select Bibliography under Timothy W. Gallwey, 2000.

the extra work. I am sure I will never make anything of it. For a while, I labor away, but my heart is not in it. At the first serious sign of problems, I carefully construct a case for dropping the project entirely. My negative self-beliefs have triumphed over both my wish for praise from my boss and the interests of the business.

There are several things that cause us to get in our own way: lack of conscious choice, automatic habits and lack of motivation are the strongest. Deteriorated strengths — strengths that have become unbalanced or tipped over into obsession — cause us great suffering. So does being unaware of the fears that come with core values. We need to explore these possible blockages and sort out antidotes to lessen their negative effects.

Letting go of negative beliefs

Clearing away wrong beliefs is a good place to start. Beliefs are just thoughts we hold on to and treat with extra reverence. There is no problem with this, unless our beliefs are just plain wrong, which they often are. Many people carry around mistaken beliefs about themselves: beliefs that stir up negative emotions and behaviors, and are guaranteed to limit their achievements and cause them unnecessary suffering. They would be far better off without these destructive passengers.

Our beliefs have power over us only because we treat them as the truth. A belief is a thought, or an opinion, that has been given the force of truth in our minds. As thoughts, they have no greater likelihood of being correct than any other thoughts. Yet once we give them the label "belief," we convince ourselves they are different and less in need of questioning. All beliefs, even false ones, contain significant amounts of emotional energy. They do not give up without a fight. Yet whether they are our own thoughts, or ones we have accepted from others, they are not matters of truth, however much we treat them as such. We do not question our beliefs nearly enough. Many of us take comfort in firm beliefs when life is difficult and the future uncertain. They feel so stable and predictable. It causes us too much unease to recognize that the ideas in which we put our trust could prove to be false.

If we are thinking clearly, we will see that a true belief will always stand up to careful scrutiny. Questioning will only make it stronger. It is the false, unthinking and outdated beliefs that will be moved out of our way. It is always worth asking ourselves, "Is this true? How do I know it is true? What evidence is there? If it used to be true, is it still to be trusted?" Beliefs need to be checked and re-checked carefully for accuracy and usefulness.

Take the belief that we should fix our eyes on some desired point in the future and let nothing get in our way. Planning our lives around a single, fixed option like this is incredibly risky. Anything other than the future outcome we believe in, we have determined is a failure.

Softening and easing our deep-seated habits is essential to accessing our unused potential, and habitual beliefs are as narrow and limiting as any other kind of habit. The largest source of negative beliefs is our ingrained habit of deficit thinking. Instead of our dreams and ambitions being used to propel us forward, we let the gap between our current state and our desires become a source of frustration and depression. Life is inherently uncertain and unpredictable. We may believe we can control things and pin the future down, but we are mistaken. As we dwell on supposed deficiencies and thwarted needs, we see anything or anyone that holds us back as an enemy. People who focus on a single direction for their future — a single role, a single kind of work, a single position in the hierarchy — risk more than they know. They plan and dream, but it does not work out that way. What is left? An individual or organization that wagers the future on a single, inflexible strategy is taking as much risk as a gambler putting his life's saving on one turn of the roulette wheel. If the bet is lost, everything may collapse. When our plans fail, we risk more than disappointment. We may find ourselves in serious trouble, especially if that one plan is all we have. Fear, frustration and hopelessness are added to the disappointment. We were so sure of the outcome, and now someone, something, has taken it away. When this happens — and it happens often — the result is always greater distress and hurt. Cheated of the desired outcome, we feel demeaned and devalued. Typically, we start to look for ways of getting our revenge, giving way to anger, jealousy and self-loathing: the most destructive emotions in any workplace. Emotional responses caused by thwarted desires are amongst the most common ways we unconsciously block our potential.

Dealing with anger

We meet anger every day around the water-cooler or the coffee machine and in bars where people congregate after work. Its favored disguise is office gossip. If you listen carefully to what people are saying, you can hear the sting of anger behind their words.

Frustration breeds anger like a rotting carcass breeds maggots. Whether it is clothed as hatred, bitterness, malicious gossip or sniping remarks, anger lets us direct our fear and misery onto others. The typical results are aggression, destruction and disdain. When we are angry, we keep thinking of all the hurtful things we want to happen to the person we are angry with. Blinded by our emotions, we lose our sense of danger and most of our ability to think clearly. In reality, we are the most likely people to be hurt or destroyed.

Organizations are full of anger. People shout and bang the doors. They curse loudly and abuse each other; sometimes openly, more often when the target of their abuse is somewhere else. They swap mean bits of gossip and nasty stories about people they dislike. People in positions of power despise those who have not made it. The latter are feared and disliked in their turn by the people below them. Upsets and unpleasant surprises are greeted with outbursts of irritation and secret glee. Customers are abused and suppliers browbeaten. Like the pressure in a steam boiler, anger produces tension and strain until it explodes in a violent outburst.

WE NEED to be careful with anger. It can feel so righteous and justified, filling us with short-term energy and providing a sense of direction. Anger clouds the judgment, undermines any ability for intelligent action and directs attention towards futile schemes for revenge. How can we find our place in the world if we are using most of our energy to feed our anger? We are blinded by our belief in the justice of our position, and entranced by the vision of our enemy writhing at our feet. We do not notice that the payoff for anger is more suffering. When we lie awake at night, seething and boiling with fury and ruining our health, we suffer more than the person against whom we are directing our emotions. Anger often backfires, leaving us exposed to ridicule and retaliation. When we are angry, the last thing we are likely to do is to question any beliefs that justify our sense of outrage. Anger, especially habitual anger, warps our judgment and skill, and corrodes our potential. Anger rarely serves a useful purpose beyond the short-term burst of adrenaline it produces. In the end, it produces nothing but misery and hatred.

Perhaps, in our natural state, anger's evolutionary purpose was to pump up our muscles in some Stone Age battle for dominance. Fistfights are strongly discouraged in modern businesses, so all that adrenaline has nowhere to go. Much of the stress we feel comes from the physical effects of a fight or flight response that cannot be turned into action. Remember the last time you got really angry? How did you feel afterwards? My guess is that you felt stressed, drained, frustrated and as miserable as before.

Restraint is a powerful antidote to anger. It is not a popular concept because it sounds puritanical. People confuse it with repression and denial. In fact, restraint is the opposite: freely acknowledging the emotions and hurt, but choosing not to act on them. By choosing restraint, we give ourselves a valuable pause for reflection and choice. Once our emotions have cooled off, we can re-establish our ability to take intelligent and skillful action. That is the hallmark of potential at work: words, thoughts and actions that resonate with skill and intelligence.

Teams and organizations also display anger. Anger can become entrenched in corporate culture. When it does, individual anger is reinforced and magnified. Some groups — perhaps whole departments — spend years conducting bitter warfare with rivals in the same organization, gleefully wrecking their initiatives and rejoicing at every failure and setback. Organizations that conduct internal battles in this way become so distracted that mere outsiders, such as customers, get scant attention. It is a quick and effective way to harm a business beyond repair.

Anger is certainly much present at times, so denying it is to deny reality. We cannot control our emotions, only the ways we express them or hold them in check. Once we acknowledge that we feel angry and look carefully to understand the source, the most useful thing we can do is let it go. Do not rehearse it, do not feed it, just acknowledge its presence and let it drop. If we continue to leave it alone in this way, it will gradually starve to death for lack of attention. If what we give most attention to increases, anything we deprive of attention will eventually wither away on its own.

The trap of jealousy

Envy and jealously also divert us from doing anything useful. Both are fed by deficit thinking: concentrating on fears of where we fall short, instead of where we might excel. When we spend time contemplating our lack of talent or ability, anyone who has what we seem to lack is bound to incite envy. Though we may feel our envy is directed to others, it always points back to us.

Jealousy's pay-off is secret harm, spitefulness and a delight in pulling people off their pedestals. It is hard to see anything useful in such an emotion. In our desire to ruin others, we take no steps to move ourselves forward. The person we envy may be brought down, but we are exactly where we were before: still as unlikely to be able to achieve what they achieved or to do what they did. The more we concentrate on wanting, the more envy we will feel. We fix our attention on the gap between our desires and our reality, and because whatever we pay most attention to will grow largest, the more envious we become, the larger that gap will appear to be. Jealousy feeds on itself, like some monstrous fungus. It fixes our minds on *other people's* potential and success, not our own. Like anger, it causes us more suffering in the long-term than we inflict on the object of our envy. It drains our ability to change and supplies grievances in the place of purpose.

There is a story of a man who sat by the fire with his daughter after a particularly bitter week at work. The little girl asked him why he was so silent and sad.

"It feels as if there are two wild animals fighting inside my head," the man said. "One wishes me to tear my boss apart and the other wants me to find the courage to change my life instead."

"Which one will win?" his daughter asked in wonder.

Her father smiled at her. "The one that I feed," he replied.

THE BEST ANTIDOTE to jealousy is *aspiration*. When we want something specific, it creates a gap between where we are and where or what we want to be. But when we acknowledge an aspiration, it provides a sense of *direction*: something to strive towards, not something to possess. This small difference is crucial. When we aim in some direction, we have a clear idea of where we are heading, but can be flexible about how we get there, taking account of the bumps and diversions along the way. If we set our hearts on a single specific outcome, anything else — however close — is a failure.

We can aspire to become as successful, or kind, or wise as anyone that we admire. There is no basis for jealousy. We are not seeking to win over others or bring them down. The more we compete, the less we will be able to focus on our own potential. Remember that whatever we give most attention to grows largest. When we compete with others, most of our attention is given to *their* success, not our own. Even in sport, trying too hard to win builds up tension and "big match nerves" to the point where performance is degraded.

Conquering self-loathing

Few things have as much power to do us harm as our own minds. An unhappy mind can cause physical sickness and disease. Depression leaves people powerless to function. Guilt can make us hate ourselves and do ourselves harm. Low self-esteem can cause us to give up trying to improve. We come to believe we cannot do better, however hard we try.

A possible payoff for this process seems to be justification for our misery. We avoid blaming ourselves by blaming others instead. We try to lessen our feelings of guilt by showing that others are responsible for our problems. In seeking to shame others, we believe we may avoid our own feelings of humiliation. It rarely works. Once again, concentrating on the gap between what we want and what we get makes the gap seem larger. The real pay-off for self-loathing is hopelessness: that creeping numbness and gradual death of any motivation to change or improve. Our minds are taken over by the enormity of the space

A SPARK FROM HEAVEN?

between what we believe we can do and what we want to achieve. Faced by that gargantuan chasm, we give up in despair.

The demon of self-loathing rarely comes alone. It usually brings anger and jealousy along. Instead of doing something positive to rise out of the place where we find ourselves, we waste whatever energy we have left on railing uselessly against fate or whoever we blame for our wretchedness. We have all encountered people who have long since abandoned any hope for themselves or their careers. They have given up the idea of leaving and trying again, so they remain in jobs that frustrate them, working for people whom they despise, and cultivating an air of world-weariness to mask their desolation. It is clear they have some ability, because they always manage to produce a performance just good enough to avoid being fired. More than that seems impossible for them, whether through lethargy or some perverse wish to contribute as little as they can.

TO COUNTER self-loathing, we need the courage to keep trying new options. Development based on opening up options and possibilities offers more choices with every day. If one option fails, there are plenty more. When we focus on ends not means, and on a commitment to fulfilling our potential instead of detailed plans on how to get there, our plans can change as circumstances change while the desired endpoint remains firm.

Management writer Margaret Wheatley tells a Mexican tale of a Quetzal bird that brings tiny drops of water in its bill to fight a huge forest fire. When the owl asks angrily what he thinks he is doing, the Quetzal replies, "I am doing my best with what I have." Inspired by this example, the animals come together and put out the fire.[8]

Summary

- ✺ We are the greatest blockage to our own potential. We stand in our own way without realizing it. Our wrong beliefs about ourselves constantly interfere with our performance and learning.
- ✺ If we treat negative beliefs as the truth, we give them power over us. They are just thoughts. Thwarted beliefs produce harmful emotions that corrupt our lives and careers.
- ✺ Anger, jealousy and self-loathing are the most common results of poor insight into how our minds work. They drain our energy and set us on a path that will produce only suffering and frustration.
- ✺ We can get back on track. There are specific antidotes. Using our potential to try fresh options makes us more flexible and open. Once we see how we have gone astray, we can quickly put things right.

---

[8] See Select Bibliography under Margaret J. Wheatley, 2002.

TEN

WHEN STRENGTHS WORK AGAINST US

> There is perhaps no phenomenon which contains so much destructive feeling as *moral indignation*, which permits envy or hate to be acted out under the guise of *virtue*.
>
> ERICH FROMM

> Strong men can always afford to be gentle. Only the weak are intent on "giving as good as they get."
>
> ELBERT HUBBARD

> A great many people think they are thinking when they are merely rearranging their prejudices.
>
> — WILLIAM JAMES

Have you ever noticed that when something really bugs you, you see it everywhere? Have you thought about this? I used to get irritated by what I considered people's laziness in thinking. Instead of taking the time to think something through, they would take a superficial position without any consideration, or dismiss an idea out of hand. It used to drive me nuts. And it was everywhere. At work, at home, in the media, in the newspapers — no one seemed able to string two coherent thoughts together.

When we become obsessive and self-righteous about something, we become hypersensitive to its opposite. I had a huge core value around the usefulness of thought, so I saw thoughtlessness everywhere. In fact, I saw almost nothing else; so I did little thinking either because my mind was taken up with complaining about how little everyone else thought. That is how it goes. The person obsessed with justice sees injustice everywhere. Someone who craves acceptance encounters little but rejection. Over-achievers live surrounded by failure and the fear of failure. The people who write to their local papers complaining about dog feces on the sidewalks (quite right too!) encounter doggie doo-doos *everywhere* they look.

None of this is real. It is an artifact of unbalanced values and habitual kinds of thinking that have become obsessive. There are always two sides to any strength. On the positive side is a benefit. On the negative is the corresponding fear. The presence of one necessitates the presence of the other. For example, if there is no failure, there can be nothing called success. Fear of failure makes us see the risk of disappointment on every side and spend our energy trying to remove it. A mindset based on avoiding failure blocks creativity and progress. Suppose that I have a strong value associated with winning or coming out on top. We usually call that value *"conquest."* Winning is only possible if losing is possible also. If I cannot lose, I cannot win. So a drive to come out on top is always accompanied by a corresponding wish to avoid losing, or even coming second. I want to win, so I have to work at avoiding the possibility of losing.

There is no problem with this so long as the balance between the opposites is maintained. But sometimes the balance breaks down and the negative side of the coin gets on top. Now my main motivation is not to win. It is to avoid losing at any cost. Instead of helping me move forward into a stronger, more enjoyable future, it traps me in the past, endlessly justifying why I did not *really* lose. It stops me from taking risks. It stops me learning from my losses, because a loss is something I cannot admit to.

Every strong value has a negative side. Where getting things back into balance is an issue, it must be dealt with as early as possible. If we allow it, the fear of the opposites of our strongest values can disable us completely. Strengths work in an identical manner. A powerful analytical ability can become unbalanced and tip over into constant agonizing over pointless details. Creativity becomes a justification for daydreaming and avoidance of reality. The drive to get things done becomes hyperactivity. A liking for being in control leads us to see chaos everywhere and keeps us exhausted trying to keep everything under control. We *have* to control everything. If we did not, our unbalanced thinking tells us that nothing would be done *properly*.

Deteriorated strengths

Whenever we combine some strength with greater access to potential, that strength is transformed, becoming freer, more flexible and more workable. We broaden our outlook and see things in a more inclusive context, adding flexibility, perspective and openness to new ideas.

When potential is *not* brought to bear on strengths, they often develop and claim attention in ways that can destroy much of the benefit. These deteriorated versions of strengths develop the opposites of the qualities that potential would have brought. Instead of becoming more flexible, free and workable, deteriorated forms are more rigid, limited in scope and doctrinaire.

Let us go back to logical analysis as an example. It has several deteriorated forms. The most common is nitpicking over-attention to detail that causes "paralysis by analysis" — the urge to analyze and re-analyze every aspect of a situation, well beyond what is needed to make decisions. Another deteriorated form is becoming pointlessly intellectual, delighting in ever more complex and obscure pieces of information. Whether it is the geek who can recite the technical details of the Starship "Enterprise," or the college professor devoting years to bitter rivalries over the correct reading of a manuscript, the pattern is the same. A third deteriorated form takes logic to its extreme and denies the possibility of human emotion or intuition, substituting blind adherence to facts, figures and scientific proofs.

Even empathy and compassion in relationships have deteriorated forms. We have probably all met the fearful do-gooder whose elaborate display of sympathy supports a towering ego and a deep longing to control others. There is a kind of fluffy bunny sentimentality that views the world through the rosiest of rose-tinted glasses; and the emotional junkie, so keen for the next fix of deep and meaningful feelings that he or she will happily stir up your worst fears or wildest hopes to come along for the ride.

Other examples quickly come to mind: the person who exercises judgment on everyone else, so all are found wanting; the adrenaline freak who rushes around in a constant frenzy of action; and the narrow minded, dogmatic fundamentalist, ready to sacrifice anyone to pursue his or her personal creed.

Spotting dysfunctional values

While our values are never good or bad, how we use them can be unskillful or unhelpful, both to us and to the people we work with. Just as with our other strengths, our strongest values — our core values — are probably those most prone to being present in dysfunctional (unhelpful and poorly adapted) forms.

Values *always* carry an emotional charge. In fact, much of the importance of a value is the emotional kick it gives us, whether towards something (motivation) or away from it (aversion). It is this emotional charge that gives values their power to influence our lives so strongly. We may have many opinions about things, but opinions are easily changed and do not push us into action. Most people who smoke share the opinion that it would be better to give up using tobacco. Yet they go on smoking, just the same. Only when their emotions are engaged — perhaps by the negative attitude towards smoking held by someone they want to impress — is there anything like a spur to action.

Organizations that allow their values to become unbalanced turn their strengths against their own best interests. They suppress dissent and demonize competitors. They no longer seek to learn from their inevitable mistakes and failures. Once they label something as a failure, they push it as far away as possible to avoid their fear.

It is important to make sure that these powerhouses of motivation and energy are working *positively*. Because our core values are so important to us, they are prone to sliding into *dysfunctional and constricted forms*, where they become rigid, inflexible and automatic. They are still powerful as motivators, and still align with our potential, but now they produce more aversion than motivation, so we spend our time and energy avoiding what we dislike, not moving towards what will benefit us. We can imagine the process as being somewhat like the immune system of the body, which can become turned against our cells instead of helping them fight off infection. When that happens, the physical result is a cancer. When our core values fall into dysfunctional, constricted forms, the result is equally cancerous to our well-being and enjoyment of life and work.

The first question to ask around a core value must be whether the behavior it is producing in us is expansive or constrictive: whether that strength — that core value — is present in a full or dysfunctional form. Any of our values that become constricted share common tendencies: they become obsessive and rigid, and they make us act in ways that are self-righteous and demanding.

Suppose someone has a powerful core value in the area of achievement and success — a common situation with senior executives. This is generally helpful for job performance and career growth. But if the value becomes constricted and dysfunctional, it will set up a cancer within that person's mind that can destroy opportunities to access potential. People in this situation become demanding

A SPARK FROM HEAVEN?

perfectionists, alienating anyone whose work is needed to build the success they crave. They hog the limelight and claim every accomplishment as their own. They drive good people away and reduce the rest to cowering submission. If the element of self-righteousness is also present, achievement can be a most unpleasant value to colleagues and subordinates.

Obsessive achievement can make people believe that the ends justify any means. The highly publicized cases of fraud by top executives in major companies show exactly this pattern. These people set themselves almost impossibly high goals. They worked long hours and devoted themselves totally to achieving their objectives. They also ignored ethical considerations, the well-being of others, and even the law, where these appeared to be obstacles to meeting their goals. In the obsessive need to demonstrate achievement, intelligent, highly educated people crossed the line into criminal behavior. Since money was usually the measure of achievement, they also displayed horrifying levels of greed.

I am sure that they believed what they were doing was justifiable — even praiseworthy. They were high achievers. They were committed and dedicated to meeting their objectives. The acceptability of the means they used was simply less important than reaching the goals they had set themselves. It may well be that they will never be able to understand what went wrong and why others found their behavior so abhorrent.

SELF-RIGHTEOUSNESS makes strong values appear self-centered and patronizing. The tendency to righteousness can tempt people to treat others in rude, unkind or even cruel ways, justifying almost any kind of ruthless treatment. We sometimes refer to this kind of behavior as macho. In reality, it is a strong value that has tipped over into cancerous growth. Unless it is caught and brought back into balance, it will gradually destroy its owner's relationships, potential and maybe even long-term career.

Righteousness can strike with just about any value, turning it from a spur to positive behavior into a reason for highly critical attitudes towards those poor unfortunates who have not yet realized the excellence of our personal value set. It numbs our humanity and allows us to justify dreadful behavior. Unfortunately, we rarely notice our own righteousness, though we are often sensitive to it in others. It is sadly amusing how often we criticize exactly the same behavior in others that we display ourselves, though probably not in relation to the same values.

Teams may become righteous about shared values too. Sharing strong values helps team cohesion, but can cause the team to become exclusive and dismissive of outsiders. There is something about fervent, shared values in a team that leads easily to collective righteousness. The shared values that everyone in the team agrees are good and sensible have shifted out of balance and become cancerous.

Diversity

Diversity is valuable mainly because it keeps us honest, so long as there is enough of it to prevent one set of values from becoming over dominant. When there are dissenting voices within the team, it is easier to listen to those outside as well. When values shift out of balance and become constricted, there is usually a sense of absolute truth about them — no more dissent will be allowed.

The world is naturally diverse, so we get diversity whether we want it or not (though some people try hard to drive it away). But it is still important. Welcoming diversity is a powerful antidote to self-righteousness. So is giving strong attention to noting where our narrowness of outlook starts to lead towards thinking anyone with different values is stupid, misguided or bad.

IF WE HAVE only one or two powerful core values, it will be easy to lose sight of anything else. Like a pair of scales with heavy weights on one end only, it will easily become unbalanced. It cannot shift smoothly towards the other end of the balance arm.

Sources of balance may be other values or different versions of the same one. Balance can also be found by deliberate efforts to explore other points of view, especially those that seem opposed. We may decide to stay with our original value set, but the experience of looking seriously at something different will help us retain perspective. We will discover these opposing values are held by people who are just as rational, sensible and well informed as we are.

The old saying that travel broadens the mind holds good for traveling around the world of values as well. The more you become aware of your own values as choices you have made, not truths you must follow, the easier it is to look at others' choices with a sense of compassion and equanimity.

Each value tends to produce its own dysfunctional versions, although same general qualities apply. All dysfunctional values tend to share:

* Narrowness of focus.

- Rigidity and inflexibility.
- An automatic exclusion of competing options.
- Self-inflicted ignorance of any other perspective.

Restoring our strengths

When someone manages to do the right thing in some tight spot, we say they display presence of mind. They stay calm and see what is needed, then do it, despite all the distractions and fear around them. It is worth taking this phrase 'presence of mind' literally. It means that the person's mind was *present* in the situation: right there, able to consider alternatives and make good decisions. Even the words people use in such situations betray that their minds are somewhere else. They may talk about something being a matter of principle, which means the current situation is linked to some abstract idea. This is the *idea* that is driving their behavior. They may feel a sense of *déjà vu*: they have been here before. Now they are reacting from the past situation they remember, not the present one.

When our strongest values are engaged, it is easy to be carried away. If we are driven somewhere else by the activity and violence of our emotions, we cannot be present in the current situation. And without presence of mind, our actions may be well intentioned, but still way off the mark.

THE FIRST STEP in bringing potential to bear on current strengths should be to explore whether we have begun to harbor any deteriorated forms of our gifts. We get so used to what works for us that we do not notice some gradual descent towards deterioration. It helps to recall the three attributes that always characterize potential:

- Greater freedom and openness

- Greater flexibility and workability
- Broader perspectives

Clearing away deteriorated forms of our strengths is like polishing away the grime and discoloration from a beautiful old piece of silver. What is restored is all the original luster and beauty of the piece.

Useful approaches include:

- Doing more reading, especially of serious topics that are well outside our normal scope of interest.
- Spending quality time trying to understand ideas that feel odd or seem to be the opposite of our habitual ways of thinking.
- Exploring radically different areas of expertise and patterns of thought. Scientists might study meditation, or theater, or spheres of knowledge they have never encountered. Non-scientists might try to understand chaos theory, particle physics, or the origin of Black Holes.

What is needed is to wake up — to find ourselves shaken and startled out of our comfort zone by people who value our strengths, but are not over impressed by them. People who will laugh at our self-justification and pomposity.

Shifting focus

The second way to bring more potential to bear on current strengths is to increase our ability to shift focus from close up and detailed to broad and holistic.

Our minds are like cameras that see the world through a series of lenses. A long lens on a camera can pick out small details in a vast landscape. It zooms in on what we want to see and excludes everything else. We also have the mental equivalent of wide-angle lenses, capable of embracing huge, panoramic views. Detail may be scarce, but we see the vast sweep of perspective in all its wonder. We even have macro lenses, like microscopes, capable of seeing tiny details in extreme close-up.

Everyone has all these lenses, so we can perceive reality at every scale, from the most detailed day-to-day plans and tasks to the broadest visions of long-term corporate destiny. Sadly, most of our lenses lie unused, while we loudly proclaim that the view provided by the one or two we keep fixed in place is the only view there is.

We get into the habit of only seeing things at a few scales — maybe only at one scale. In time, we cannot recall anything else. Instead of our minds being like highly professional photographers, with lenses for every purpose, they become like people taking snaps with simple, disposable cameras. The difference is that the happy holidaymaker with the cheap camera knows that it is not going to give professional results. We take our fixed focus, single speed, and single-lens cameras and assume that the pictures we get are the best around.

"Zooming"

The antidote to this situation is to cultivate "zooming," deliberately shifting focus from close up to the widest diorama (and everything in between), and carefully noticing what appears at each scale.

Zooming is one of the most powerful techniques for accessing greater potential. It uses all the skills, experience and knowledge we have built up, and adds a way to deliberately step beyond the habitual and open up more freedom, flexibility and perspective. Comfort is enhanced by stretch and rigidity is replaced by the openness to try new things and learn by the result.

This is not necessarily an easy activity. At the highest vantage points, which offer the most panoramic overviews, vertigo is a constant hazard. It is easy to feel dizzy and disoriented. It is also scary. We may fear we will fall and hurt ourselves. We long to get back to the flatter, safer ground. If we are comfortable on the peaks, detailed close ups might make us strain and squint, as we try to see at ranges far more detailed than we find comfortable.

That is why it is best to take it slowly. This is a progressive technique. There is no need to strain unduly or push ourselves beyond what we can handle. Once we build some flexibility and sense of ease, we can always go a little farther the next time. The extra perspectives are always there.

Summary

- ✵ When we become obsessive and self-righteous about something we value, we become hypersensitive to its opposite.
- ✵ Values can slip into constrictive, dysfunctional formats. When they do, they produce limiting, demanding kinds of behavior, often characterized by unpleasant self-righteousness and careless cruelty.
- ✵ Diversity of values is the best antidote to this kind of narrowness, especially in teams. While team cohesiveness increases when members share a few strong values, such teams easily become exclusive and dismissive of outsiders and their opinions.
- ✵ Whenever we combine a strength with greater access to potential, that strength is transformed,

becoming freer, more flexible and more workable. When potential is *not* brought to bear on strengths, they develop and claim attention in ways that can destroy much of their benefit.

* Taking action to broaden our interests and attention helps repair damaged strengths. So does deliberately changing our perspectives.
* The presence of a strength always brings along the corresponding fear. When strengths become unbalanced, we concentrate on the fear and lose sight of the benefits.
* Presence of mind is a universal antidote to most of these difficulties. When we are truly present, not away somewhere chewing over our opinions and grievances, it is easy to see when we are losing perspective.

ELEVEN

THE ART OF POSSIBILITY

> The world is the sum total of our vital possibilities.
>
> — ORTEGA Y GASSET

> The future is not some place we are going to, but one we are creating. The paths are not to be found, but made, and the activity of making them changes both the maker and the destination.
>
> —JOHN SCHAAR

> The phrases that men hear or repeat continually end by becoming convictions and ossify the organs of intelligence.
>
> — JOHANN GOETHE

There are four essential ingredients in the process of *realizing* potential: motivation, recognition, opportunity and, above all, choice. We have to want to do it and be willing to make sufficient effort for long enough to get results. We need to recognize our potential through exploring possibilities and options, and making sure that we are not missing anything important. We will gain the opportunities we need only by seeking them out and persuading others to support us. Most important of all, we must start to make different choices in areas of our lives where we are probably coasting along in our comfort zone.

If we want to gain access to our potential, we *must* be ready to try new approaches and test out fresh options. That is where our potential is. Unfortunately, most of us simply stay on comfortable ground.

This has puzzled me for a long time. Why and how do we lose that curiosity and eagerness to try new things that we all possessed as children?

Rule Number 6

In their book *The Art of Possibility*[9], Rosamund and Benjamin Zander introduce us to *Rule Number 6*: "Don't take yourself so goddam seriously." Asked what the other five rules are, their response is: "There aren't any."

Rule Number 6 is an important clue. Whenever I start to take myself *really* seriously, I find that I become deeply worried about what others think of me. I want to control things. I want life to be predictable. After all, given how important I am, it is only right that the world should do what I want.

Children do not take themselves so seriously — at least until adults convince them that it is important. I guess we learn it sometime in our teens. As a teenager, I took myself so seriously that it hurt. I fretted about how I

---

[9] See Select Bibliography under Rosamund and Benjamin Zander, 2000.

looked, whether I was behaving in ways that friends would approve, and especially whether girls would suddenly start to notice my undoubted sexual magnetism — something that has unaccountably failed to this day. I took my opinions so seriously that I never lost an opportunity to preach to anyone fool enough to listen. I decided what my life was going to be — only it never was. Like almost all teenagers, I was so serious about expressing my individuality, that I behaved and dressed exactly like everyone else in my group.

Before you laugh at me too much, try to recall what you were like at that age. Embarrassing, huh? Now think about the most uptight, risk-averse and conventional person you know. How seriously does he or she take himself or herself? *That* seriously? Wow!

"Don't take yourself so goddam seriously" should be written on the wall in every office and boardroom. It would save us all from making total fools of ourselves on a regular basis.

The gift of uncertainty

You would think that by this stage in the evolution of the human species we would have caught on that our world is:

1. A uncertain place; and
2. Totally outside our control.

Not a bit of it! We spend large amounts of our time, especially in the world of work, fruitlessly trying to control things to produce predictability and stability. I have reached the view that this is the other main reason why we often avoid new possibilities and stay in our comfort zones. It is just too unpredictable and unstable outside.

Management is all about predictability. We set budgets, hold audits and submit regular reports in the cause of producing a stable, foreseeable world. When the universe goes its own sweet way and ignores what we have done, we do not admit that our attempts were worthless. We name the gaps between our pointless attempts and reality, calling them *variances* or *performance gaps*, and try to account for them as well. We set up programs of cost control instead of practicing frugality, and replace commonsense dealings with complex rules and regulations.

The more we try to pin things down and create a sense of security, the more insecure we will feel. I guarantee it. Remember that when we become obsessive about something, all we see is the opposite? The more we try to keep things under control, the more chaos we will see around us. The more we chase after predictability, the more uncertainty we will find. The more we fear change, the more changes there will be to fear.

THE ANTIDOTE to fear of uncertainty is letting go. Instead of trying to predict and control, we can enjoy the constant surprises that come along. Instead of facing the future with a grim determination to have things our way, we can relax and look ahead with interested curiosity.

If we do that, we will make an intriguing discovery: our only true safety lies in the wealth of possibilities that come along. If one thing fails to work, there will be another along in a moment. If we make a mistake, we can try something else instead. After all, making mistakes is easy. Everyone does it all the time. Our mistakes are no worse than everyone else's.

Because we take ourselves so goddam seriously, we inflate minor setbacks into disasters and daily decisions into agonizing dilemmas. Real matters of life and death are astonishingly rare, yet we seem to encounter them all the time. Could it be that we are only frightening ourselves with all this nonsense? As small children, maybe we were scared of monsters under our beds or nameless horrors that lurked in the dark. As adults, we are far too sophisticated for that. We fear our own lives.

It is a common misconception that potential is a fixed point somewhere in the future. We speak of someone having potential for a senior position. Perhaps — even more specifically — of someone having the potential to be, say, CEO. This implies that his or her potential will *only* be realized by reaching that particular post.

It makes no sense to fasten our expectations and hopes on such a *fixed* point in the future, especially without truly understanding the situation we have convinced ourselves we desire. If it does not work out, the sense of failure can be hard to live with. Even if it does, what we so earnestly desired might not live up to our hopes. It is far better to review many options and be constantly alert to all opportunities that arise, sometimes unexpectedly. The waste of commitment, energy and ability from unmet expectations can be enough to undermine the future of a whole corporation. The best people leave and those who remain feel cheated of something they had come to see as a right. Their frustration leads to lower commitment and inferior performance.

It is simply not necessary. Uncertainty is a wonderful gift. Bad things change, as well as good ones. We are never condemned to a rigid future. By replacing fixed expectations with a constant exploration of what will allow us to make that next step forward and build an even stronger contribution, the future will always contain more hopeful options than we can utilize.

Once we are free from a fixed set of expectations, we have the flexibility to seize opportunities as they come. Knowing what we already do well, and where we can still develop, promotes self-confidence. Instead of seeing our lives as events that happen to us, we can view life as an outcome we are bringing about, and ask ourselves what we are doing and what results will be generated.

If we align ourselves with the fundamental values that we hold most dear and the natural gifts that we have, the result is an alert, strongly motivated and powerfully optimistic viewpoint.

A universe of possibilities

Potential is possibility and possibility is everywhere. We all have abundant talents — far more than we use — and can develop still more. If we become explorers of our own lives and careers, we will push past the assumed barriers of existing knowledge and comfort that hem us in, and find new lands and possibilities. Nothing that is already in place need be lost. There is no choice to be made between proven successes and unproven potential. It is all part of our potential, to be realized and used just as we wish.

This exploration is well worth our time and trouble. All living creatures are programmed to grow. We unwittingly produce many of the ills in our lives and careers by limiting this natural growth. Once we recognize that potential is usable and extendable in almost infinite directions, we are no longer held within imagined boundaries that shut out vast areas of success and enterprise. We can find more ways to make successful contributions, more scope for stepping up to whatever challenges arise, more options and possibilities for feeling good about ourselves, and new ways to let others feel good about us. It takes effort, but it lies within us to achieve. We just need to set about it with courage and commitment.

Developing our potential will require determination and motivation. We have to make the effort. The good news is that, once we are on the right track, it will be the kind of effort that leaves us exhilarated and excited. Playing requires effort, but you will not find many children refusing to play because they have to exert themselves. Of course, there are some people who have developed strong habits of laziness and lethargy. If we value lounging on the couch more than developing our potential, that is our choice and we must live with the results.

THE MOST COMMON causes of fear about developing potential are concerns about making mistakes and looking foolish, and anxiety about somehow losing what we already have.

No one likes to seem foolish or stupid. That is why the instantaneous response to mistakes in most organizations is some effort at concealment. Mistakes may also attract ridicule or punishment in some work environments. No wonder that people who work there are afraid to move away from whatever solid ground they can find. They have practical reasons for being afraid. In the same situation, we would all be apprehensive. Obedience is more of a requirement than many organizations care to admit. Whether it is called "not rocking the boat" or "following correct policies" it is still obedience.

Despite claims of commitment to development and learning, it sometimes seems that organizations, and some of the people around us, have much more invested in keeping us the way we are. Even our closest colleagues and friends may treat any changes in our behavior with deep suspicion. Before we become paranoid about this, let us see it from their position. It is not really malice or some attempt to hold us back. We all live in a web of relatedness. Pull on one part of the web and all the other parts around it will vibrate. As we change, so must the people who deal with us. Maybe they have not chosen to do that right now.

Fear is always critical and judgmental. It upsets our perceptions and gets all the perspectives wrong. Every shadow is a lurking assassin. Every colleague is whispering about us behind our backs. The antidote is to remember that these are just thoughts. Fear is simply thoughts and imagination. If we make the effort to look around at the people who frighten us, and try to understand what is driving them to do what they do — not to condemn, but to look with compassion on *their* fears — we will get our anxieties back into perspective. As Mark Twain said, "Some of the worst things in my life never happened."

Fear also makes us blame others and ignore our own contribution to whatever is making us afraid. In many years of working with people to realize their potential, I have found that the single greatest obstacle to success is our unwillingness to face our own fears and accept full accountability for our lives. We are all guilty of it from time to time. It is so much easier to seek out scapegoats, or to wait for someone else to make an effort on our behalf.

Naturally, if the results are not what we want, we feel justified in complaining loudly that we have not been given a fair deal!

The power of probing questions

One of the best ways to handle fearful imaginings is to face them and see what they can reveal to us. There are many imagined terrors that will block our development, if we let them. They often surface as rhetorical questions: ones that need no answer, since it is obvious what that answer will be. A positive way to work with such questions is to take each as a serious request for information. Much of our potential can be locked away behind these questions.

WE DISTRACT and dismay ourselves with rhetorical questions like: "How can I develop my potential when my life is such a mess?" A question like that deserves a careful answer. If we push it away, or treat it like an enemy, we will never find what it can reveal to us. We should not allow it to be an excuse. We should stop and look at it and explore what it is telling us. Perhaps starting to deal with whatever makes our life feel a mess is precisely the way to start exploring and accessing our potential. We have to start somewhere. Why not there?

Here are some typical questions that I have been given as excuses for inaction, or reasons why someone could not possibly work towards realizing their potential. They all begin with "how?" so my suggestion is to try making a list of possible answers for any of the questions that apply. Answer the "how?" with practical suggestions. If you cannot think of any, your next step is clear: go out and look for some.

How can I develop my potential when…
- …I hate my job so much?
- …I feel so disappointed with my performance?
- …there is so much stress and anxiety in my life?
- …the people around me do not support me?
- …I have no sense of purpose or direction?
- …I do not know what it is?
- ….my career has lost all momentum?
- …even thinking about it makes me feel depressed?
- …my qualifications are so poor?
- …I might be about to lose my job?
- …I already have so many other things to do?

These questions are not asked with the expectation of an answer. We only expect others to murmur something reassuring like, "of course, you are right. No one could expect you to develop against that handicap." Try taking each question as a *question*, not as an objection. Treat them as genuine questions worthy of thoughtful answers. Set out to answer them. Explore how you might develop and access your potential even if the last part of the question feels true. You may find that it is not.

Our minds are good at creating paper tigers and terrifying creatures hidden under the bed. As adults we tend to look down on the fears we had as children, but it does not mean that they have gone away. The mechanism still works well, but now we clothe our imaginary monsters in more realistic ways.

Because we can imagine something, it does not make it *likely*. Attempting to plan ways around the infinite number of terrors and threats our minds can dream up will immobilize us permanently. Of course things may go wrong. Events may upset our plans, or what we achieve may prove less desirable than we thought. Life is like that. We need to let it go and move on.

The importance of not knowing

Our culture has little time for *not* knowing. Every news program, newspaper and magazine is filled with the words of people who claim to be in the know. Experts are everywhere, telling us that they understand exactly what has happened, what will happen or — most frequently of all — what ought to happen. They all have points of view and push them as hard as they can.

A useful way of grasping the vital importance of *not* knowing is to see it as always keeping an open mind. Our habits work to close our minds to all possibilities except those that fit either past actions or our present comfort zone. If we are to step past our habits into our potential, we need to encounter all situations with a truly open mind.

Knowing closes your mind down. It tells you: "This is right; that is wrong." With knowing, there is no need for exploration. Since I know two and two make four, I do not need to carry out any experiment to test it. What is more, if I did and found the answer was five, I would assume I had made a mistake. Instead of asking myself "How did that happen? I wonder what is going on here?" I would be criticizing myself for getting my sums wrong.

Buddhists have a concept they call *Beginner's Mind*. It is the state of mind of someone who knows they know nothing about the subject and is therefore open to see whatever is there. The expert does not look, because he or she already assumes knowledge of what will be found. While this makes for speed and efficiency, it severely lessens the scope for creativity or innovation. In the beginner's mind there are infinite possibilities. In the expert's mind, few survive the weight of assumption that knowledge and experience have placed on them.

Once, long ago, a group of Athenians was trying to flatter the philosopher Socrates. "You have such marvelous knowledge," they cooed. "You know everything." Socrates was far too wise to fall for such nonsense, and far too concerned with the truth to give an answer that was not direct and honest. "The only thing I know," he said, "is that I know nothing." What he meant was the expert's knowing: the kind of knowing that is final and fixed, and that ignores further exploration because it assumes it knows the answer in advance. Socrates' *Beginner's Mind* allowed him to see events and concepts clearly and without prejudice. Plato's accounts of the great man's discussions with his disciples make for tough reading. Socrates never let an unconscious assumption pass unnoticed — and never let anyone get away with claiming he already knew. In this quest to connect with our potential, it is also best for us to assume we know *nothing* finally and definitively. All our options should remain open.

When we take our assumptions and opinions as some kind of truth, we have created an atmosphere that will never lead to the development of our potential. We need instead to look carefully and deeply, opening our minds to see what is truly there. *It is that simple.* Just sit and look clearly at your work, your life or your career, free from all the habits and expectations that normally obscure plain vision. Work at opening up your mind to explore and realize the potential that is there, hidden by the outdated knowledge, outworn habits and all the tired assumptions we carry around in our heads.

Our habits continually urge us to buy into old patterns of thinking and actions that limit our potential and constrict the possibilities open to us. They cause us to fear new ideas and unexpected possibilities. They hurry us past awkward questions about whether things really are as we have been told. Like parents worn out with a toddler's questions, our habits snap back: "Things are as they are. No point in asking why."

Living on the edge

We will always do our best work right at that fruitful and scary edge where the future becomes the present, and where possibilities are either made real, or discarded forever. These in-between states are essential for our growth. Whenever we stand in this vibrant, scary position, all possibilities and potential are open to us. Everything is up for grabs. The fixed, past state can be broken up. The future state has not yet been made solid or definite. This is where all change and growth lie. Too often, we are so afraid of uncertainty and not knowing that we let predetermined views and opinions take over. We try to fix the future into the outworn patterns of the past and feel aggrieved when this approach does not work.

IT IS A MISTAKE to think of potential as something special that we use only in the most exciting and rarified aspects of our working lives. Potential is nothing special. It is a normal, daily part of who we are. It works for the dull aspects of our lives as well as the exciting ones. Most of the time our lives are not that exciting. We have many things to do that are humdrum at best. If we want to access more of our potential, we have to find ways that work in the routine parts of our working lives. We have to pay close attention to daily choices. More than anything else, we have to avoid automatic decisions wherever and whenever we can.

A successful man was dying. In his life, he had built more than a dozen thriving businesses and earned huge rewards. Before the man died, his grieving son pleaded to be told the secret of his success. "I do whatever works," his father replied. "If it stops working, I do something different." That should be how we act — doing whatever works and being ready to change as soon as it is not helpful anymore.

Summary

* The route to realizing potential demands a willingness to try new approaches and open up fresh possibilities. Whatever blocks this works against our best interests.
* We often take ourselves much too seriously. This causes us stay uptight, risk-averse and conventional in our thinking and actions.
* Trying to make the world a predictable place is a waste of time and effort. The more we concentrate in increasing our security, the more aware we will be of the insecurity around us. The only true source of security lies in being willing to bend to events, and finding different paths whenever we get blocked.
* Fixing our eyes on some desirable place in the future, and placing all our hopes and dreams on getting there, will be virtually certain to lead to nothing but disappointment. It is far better to be alert to all the opportunities and possibilities that come

along. Fixed sets of expectations tie us down and limit our perspectives.
- Possibility is everywhere. We can extend our potential in every direction, once we overcome the fear that holds us back. The best antidote to fear is remembering that fears are only thoughts and most of them will prove to be completely unfounded.
- We can make our fears into powerful tools to uncover potential if we treat the questions they raise in our minds as serious points for enquiry, not objections to progress.
- Uncertainty means not knowing. But *not* knowing is far more valuable in searching for potential than any amount of prior knowledge. Keeping an open mind is a prerequisite for realizing potential.
- We need to be willing to live on the edge between present and future, and between comfort and stretch, where past patterns can be broken up to let new patterns take their place.

TWELVE

WHY SPOIL THE HABITS OF A LIFETIME?

> "Curious things, habits. People themselves never knew they had them."
> — AGATHA CHRISTIE

> "Consciousness is a phase of mental life which arises in connection with the formation of new habits. When habit is formed, consciousness only interferes to spoil our performance."
> — W. R. INGE

> "Habits are cobwebs at first, cables at last."
> — CHINESE PROVERB

Let us try a little word association test. I will say a word and you say the first word that comes into your head. Ready...? Habits. Hands up all those who said bad. Okay, I will include variations on the same idea, like nasty or disgusting for those of you with vivid imaginations or guilty secrets.

Habits have a really bad press. They are nearly always linked to all the fun things in life that stern moralists lecture us about avoiding. If you say that someone is a creature of habit, it is not a compliment. Yet habits *work*. They are a natural and essential part of our lives. Evolution has programmed us that way.

OUR ABILITY to form habits developed because of its evolutionary value. By making routine actions automatic, habits free our minds for other things. We have been designed to be efficient creators of habit — and just as efficient at pushing these habits out of our consciousness, while letting them operate at full strength. Can you imagine if we dealt with every part of our day as if it was the first time? Life would slow to a crawl. All our energy would be taken up by working out how to wash, or make breakfast, or find the right road to work. Habits make our lives smoother and less demanding.

Remember the sudden jolt when you realize that you have been driving for five or ten miles, but have no recollection of what you were doing? You know you have negotiated junctions and traffic lights, avoided people crossing the road, and kept a wary eye on other drivers. You hastily look in the mirror, but there do not seem to be piles of wrecked vehicles or maimed pedestrians behind you. There are no traffic cops on your tail. Your automatic habits kept you functioning, while your conscious mind attended to something else. Habits *work*.

A SPARK FROM HEAVEN?

They do not arise by chance either. No one forms a habit out of something that did not work the first time and has never worked since. They are there because we found by experience that they succeed. We form habitual, automatic forms of behavior because we dealt with something successfully. The next time it occurred, we tried the same response and it worked again, so a habit started to grow. Our habits always represent past successes. That is why they feel so useful to us. That is why we all get so attached to them. Of course what works depends on what we rate as success. Even the strangest habits we will ever come across have been put there because they produced what was intended.

My Burmese cat loves attention. If I do not give him attention when he wants it, he will try to make me notice him; and if yowling — Burmese never meow, they wail like demented banshees — or patting my arm fails, he has found that knocking a delicate ornament off a high shelf, scratching the newest furniture, or jumping from the floor into the small of my back and hanging there by his claws, always works.

Ask any parent how long it takes little children to learn that being naughty gets attention much more quickly than being good. If attention equals success, *anything* that produces attention is successful. The boss who habitually shouts and terrorizes his staff behaves like that because it delivers enough of what he wants. The folk who spread gossip about co-workers, make long, personal telephone calls on work time, or jump the line in the staff restaurant, do what they do because they have found that it gives them what they want often enough to be worth repeating.

A SPARK FROM HEAVEN?

THERE WOULD NOT be a problem if our evolutionary tendency to create and use habits stayed in the more mundane parts of our lives — like turning sharp left into the elevator whenever we notice anyone from Accounts coming along the corridor — but it does not. The same process operates in *all* aspects of what we do. We form habits around how we work, how we deal with other people, how we react to problems, and even how we think. We do it quickly and efficiently, pushing the habits below the level of conscious thought, but still letting them function. Since we are often in a hurry at work — too much to do and never enough time — we let our habits take over to lessen the pressure. We fly on automatic pilot whenever we can.

Evolution designed us to live in the Stone Age, so when it came to fitting us to live and work in the world as it is today, it screwed up big time. Evolution in animal species happens over millions of years, so slowly that it cannot be seen in any single lifetime. That offers plenty of time for evolution to make a few million mistakes and still come out on top. "Bit sad about the dinosaurs, but hey, never mind. I am sure I saw a few mammals lying around on the workbench somewhere."

That will not work for evolving appropriate behavior if you have got a pack of wolves sniffing your butt and thinking about dinner. You have got to be able to learn what works, and what does not, pretty damn quickly.

Imagine our Stone Age ancestors trying to get some fast food. Theirs was faster than ours because it ran away. Pretty often, they had to run away too, if they did not want to be eaten by something big and nasty. If you are a Stone Age hunter who has got to find food and shelter, while surviving to become the ancestor of corporate public relations executives, you need all the help you can get. Anything that works without you having to think about it is just about your favorite behavior. The process of evolution in individual behavior quickly grew to be so swift that it is over before we notice it.

Stepping beyond our habits

If habits are so useful, why are they such a hindrance if we want to develop our potential?

It is not their usefulness that is the difficulty; it is their *unconsciousness* and *tendency to solidify*. Like the tiny, soft-bodied creatures that build coral, habits start off small and flexible, and end up by building massive reefs all around our minds. Inside the reefs, the water feels quiet and friendly. Outside we think it is going to be rough and stormy. There may be sharks.

If we are to develop our potential, we must go outside the reef of habits that mark the boundaries of our comfort zone. There is nothing wrong with those habits. They have worked for us. Now it is time to step over them and go into the wider world of our unused potential. Our fears do not know what is going to be out there, so they invent monsters and scary beasts.

For some of us, it is not only fear that holds us back. It is laziness. "Take it easy," our habits murmur. "Give yourself a break. No sense in going out there where there are big waves to handle. The water is calm in here. You just lie back and think about something else. It will all turn out well, you will see." Caught between fear and laziness, is it any wonder that we usually give in? Gradually our habits stop being helpful aids to get us through the day. They calcify and harden into boundary reefs that limit our thinking and get to direct most of what we see and how we react. We do not have to make conscious choices any longer. It is jarring to try to break through the reefs of habitual thoughts and actions. We do not like to be jarred.

SOMETIMES we make mistakes. We are not born with an instruction manual for life. Despite all the helpful advice from parents, teachers and elders, we must make our own way in the world, doing the best we can and quite often getting things wrong. Messing up a few times would not be a big deal if it were not for our innate tendency to fix on mental actions and make them habitual as well. Thinking on a habitual basis can turn the odd mistake into an ongoing life and work catastrophe.

The most deeply unconscious habits we have are habits of thinking. They are buried so far down that it takes an effort to see them for what they are — simply another set of habits. We have lived with them for a long time, probably since we were kids. We feel they are part of who and what we are. We do not want to check them out. "Hey there, that is my mind you are messing with! Back off, buddy!"

IF WE WANT to develop our potential, we must step over even our most fondly held and successful mental habits and try some new types of thinking. There is no other way. Habits of thinking block us from seeing things in new ways or finding fresh ideas. No new ideas, no learning. No learning, no access to anymore potential.

Here is how the mind works. Our brains are extremely selective, always focusing on what seems most important and ignoring the rest. That is how we can stand in a crowded street talking to a friend, tuning out the rest of the noise. It is a natural, unconscious process. It stops us from being overwhelmed by all the things going on around us. Evolution has also given us the ability to form concepts and put things into categories, so the first thing our brains do with whatever seems important is sort out what *kind* of thing it is. Is it a *food* thing, or a *lust* thing, or a *look at this* thing, or a *run like hell* thing? Once we have a category, the brain starts scanning the memory banks for ways of responding.

Our brains choose what to focus on *and* how to think about it. Well, we believe *we* do, but in reality nearly all of this goes on way below the level of consciousness. By the time the brain has grabbed our attention, paused the sexy movie we were playing in our heads, and told us there is something out there we have to deal with, it has already dumped what it saw as irrelevant and categorized and sifted the rest. Now it is ready to present us with the situation, plus a nice set of instructions.

"Hey," it says. "Sorry to interrupt, but she would never actually — okay, sorry, sorry. Look, here is one of those situations you do have to deal with. I have checked it out and it is nothing too difficult. You already know about this kind of thing. To save you time, I have talked with Memory and recalled the usual — no, make that best — way to deal with it." Like the perfect English butler, your brain presents you with the problem *and* the answer, laid out neatly on a silver tray. All you have to do is nod, get on with following the instructions, and look forward to pressing the play button on the movie.

What matters is to see that the way we think most of the time is based on a set of habits that *we* put there. That is what happens when we grow up. We stop using thinking about what happens to us and use *memory* and *habit* instead. It is so easy and familiar. Much of the time, it works just fine — as long as we do not want to do anything different. It is like the day after a really good party. You hope you can walk around and function more or less like a human being — once you have made it out of bed — but you know you definitely cannot cope with anything beyond the basics.

Flying on automatic pilot

It is so tempting to allow our habits to function as much as possible. They feel comforting and stable. We easily convince ourselves that anything new will be too difficult. Since we tend to blame things and people 'out there' for the frustrations in our lives, we may also reckon there is no need for us to change. As long as we give no attention to the part we play in the upsets and setbacks we have experienced, we have no need to improve anything. Of course, even if we *could* do something about the stumbling blocks "out there," the ones within us will remain — ready to cause more havoc and suffering.

THE OTHER PROBLEM with our habits is they rapidly fade from our conscious minds. They become automatic. Like old friends and wallpaper, we do not notice them anymore. They are just there: active, busy and completely hidden. Habits make our decisions for us without engaging any conscious thought process.

A SPARK FROM HEAVEN?

Habit leads us to *avoid* fresh options in favor of the *tried and true* (also known as the *stale, washed up* and *obsolete*). Habit that has solidified blocks learning. Learning is the only route to developing greater access to our potential, and learning requires new behaviors and possibilities to operate. Without learning, there will be no access to new talents. That is why solidified, unconscious habits are such a significant blockage to accessing potential.

Even successful habits eventually lose their appropriateness as events change and new responses are called for. But habits cling on long after their usefulness has gone. Our once-successful choices fail — a result we usually attribute to someone or something outside ourselves and we do not notice the habits, so we miss the part they play in causing the difficulty. Letting these habits become automatic and take the controls is a sure road to self-inflicted harm.

YOU WOULD THINK that if things were not going too well, we would have worked out that repeating current behavior is the most likely means to keep them that way. After all, doing the same thing and expecting a different result each time is one of the definitions of madness. By that reckoning, most of us are terminally insane. We are so trapped by our unconscious, automatic behaviors and calcified responses that we continually repeat ourselves, hoping each time for different results. We are sleepwalking through life, not noticing that if we always do the same thing, we will always get the same result. To get a different result, we *must* do something different to bring it about. We must wake up and tell our habits to get out of the way.

We must take control again and start learning better ways to direct our lives.

There was once a laboratory where scientists trained rats to run mazes in return for food. Later they ran an experiment where student volunteers ran bigger mazes for food. The experiments ran all week and on Friday, when the experiment was over, the scientists and the rats went home. The students came back secretly, broke into the laboratory and went on running the empty maze all weekend, just in case there was food next time.

Here is the bottom line. Over time, we gather a set of habits, beliefs and opinions around us. Pretty soon we come to see them as solid. They slip below the level of our consciousness, but still define what we think we can and cannot do — and what we cannot even bring ourselves to try.

Habits become the major factors that affect our working lives. We fall asleep at the wheel and give the direction of our careers to an automatic set of instructions that we probably never properly examined or evaluated. This internal software pre-programs us to behave in specified ways. So long as we let this continue, we *cannot* learn and we *cannot* develop potential. We are stuck in a rut, repeating the past, running on tramlines. We cannot grow until we take control again.

A lot of us run most of our lives on habitual patterns of thinking and action, at work and at home. These habits are not harmful in themselves. There are not wrong. The best of them are useful and work just fine. But many are left over from a different past. They are harmful because they have solidified and become repetitive and automatic. These habits ought to be put out to grass as a reward for good and faithful service. We are putting ourselves at risk. We go on using these automatic responses, while constant change makes them irrelevant and useless.

Our habitual patterns provide a false sense of security and stability. They become thick shells that insulate us from the possibilities and challenges around us. In trying to avoid the discomfort and effort of change, we lose the gains of development and growth.

Recently I was in a shop in a small town near my home. By the door was a large turtle made from rusty scrap metal. (Alright, I am a strange person who goes into some odd shops. But if I had not, I would have missed a good idea). There was a printed notice stuck to the turtle's shell. I bent down to read what it said. It read: "Turtles only make progress when they stick their necks out." How true.

We humans are said to be smarter than turtles. Yet when we recognize we are stuck in repetitive situations and continual disappointment, our clever reaction is to get back in our shells and wallow in frustration and demotivation. We are not going to stick our necks out and learn anything new, no sir. That is way too risky. We will just go on harming our own prospects and allowing our habits to block us again and again.

Summary

- Our ability to form habits developed because of its evolutionary value.
- We have been designed to be efficient creators of habit, pushing them out of our consciousness, while letting them operate at full strength.

- Our habits always represent past successes. We form habitual, automatic forms of behavior because we dealt with something successfully, tried the same response next time and it worked again. That is how habits grow and why they feel so useful to us.
- It is not the usefulness of habits that is the difficulty; it is their unconsciousness and tendency to solidify.
- The most deeply unconscious habits we have are habits of thinking. They are buried so far down that it takes an effort to see them as simply another set of automated responses.
- If we want to develop our potential, we must go outside the reef of habits that marks the boundaries of our comfort zone. We must step over our most fondly held mental norms and try some new types of thinking.
- Habit that has solidified blocks learning. Learning is the only route to developing greater access to our potential and learning requires new behaviors and possibilities to operate. Without learning there will be no access to new potential.

THIRTEEN

YOU ARE WHAT YOU CHOOSE

> People are always blaming their circumstances for what they are. I do not believe in circumstances. The people who get on in this world are the people who get up and look for the circumstances they want, and, if they cannot find them, make them.
>
> — GEORGE BERNARD SHAW

> We who lived in concentration camps can remember the men who walked through the huts comforting others, giving away their last piece of bread. They may have been few in number, but they offer sufficient proof that everything can be taken from a man but one thing: the last of the human freedoms — to choose one's attitude in any given set of circumstances, to choose one's own way.
>
> — VIKTOR E. FRANKL

Our destiny is made of choices. What will happen for us depends on the choices we made in the past and their consequences in the future. Careful, conscious choices produce positive outcomes; hurried, poor choices often lead to regrets. Choice offers us options — options to respond differently than we have responded in the past, to try new things. As Viktor Frankl discovered in Auschwitz, choice is the ultimate human freedom. Our knee-jerk reactions block any opportunity to learn and grow. Making conscious choices restores our freedom to choose our own way.

One of the many oddities about the human race is our reluctance to deal with options. We do not like having too many choices. It gets confusing and it makes us anxious. Every alternative means another opportunity for making the wrong decision and messing things up. Many of us are more concerned about not being wrong than we are about being right.

My wife hates shopping — any kind of shopping — while I rather enjoy it. She goes out with a determined expression to buy, say, a skirt and comes back later with a pair of shoes. I duly admire the shoes and ask innocently, "What happened about the skirt?" At least six times out of ten the answer is the same, "There were just hundreds of choices. Far too many. I couldn't face trying to find what I wanted." And the shoes? They were probably on sale, a few in a prominent display, and the only real decision was whether they felt comfortable.

We are all like this. Too much choice feels worse than none at all. That is why we let our habits narrow down the alternatives to one or two familiar ones. It is much less stressful.

For the committed seeker after potential, every choice is a priceless opportunity. *The most important step in realizing potential is to re-establish conscious choice in place of all those automatic, habitual decisions.* This will not just give us back our ability to find fresh options to replace worn out habits; it will permanently increase our opportunities to learn, now and in the future. Realizing potential through your work is not a once-and-for-all action; it is a way of living that makes everything you do more vibrant, more alive and more fun.

The most seductive trap comes from automatically limiting our options to save ourselves time or effort. Fewer options lead to fewer possibilities and possibility is the fabric from which potential is made. We need to be like children, endlessly curious about everything and always wondering if there is a better way.

HERE IS the beauty of using conscious choice as the road to find and realize potential. We do it all the time. Our lives are made up of hundreds of thousands of small choices. Every day we make dozens of new ones. Even in the most monotonous parts of our work, there are choices to be made, if only we wake ourselves up and realize they are there. And every *conscious* choice — every single one — contains the possibility for allowing us to connect with a little bit more of our potential.

My first introduction to the importance of choosing the attitude we take to events came nearly twenty years ago. A senior executive in a large hospital complex called and asked me to work with the Head of Nursing Operations. She had unexpectedly handed in her resignation and was in a highly emotional state. Further enquiries showed the reason. A group of large hospitals was being formed into a hospital trust, and the post of Head of Nursing Services for the trust had been advertised. The lady I was asked to see was considered by everyone to be the obvious choice for the position, but things had not gone that way. She had interviewed poorly, and the appointing committee gave the job to her deputy instead. Not surprisingly, she was extremely upset.

I agreed to talk to her the next day to see what I could do. When she came to my office, she spent more time crying than talking. She had fixed all her expectations on this job and viewed it as the crowning point of her career. If she could not have it, she could not go on. That was the immediate, instinctive choice she made. It is one many of us make when we are disappointed: "If I cannot have what I want, I would prefer to have nothing."

To be honest, I had little idea what I could do, but she seemed so helpless that I thought we should try to understand what had gone wrong. I therefore arranged another session and we began to explore the reasons for her poor interview. I was in for another surprise. As far as I could see, she had done just about as well as she could. I had not been present, of course, but I could not see anything obvious that was wrong. I phoned the Head of Administration at the hospital, who had been at the interviews, and he confirmed what she was telling me. She had interviewed as he had expected, he told me. She had all the qualifications and experience, but something had been missing. There was no spark of excitement. The committee was resigned to giving her the job, against their real wishes, until her deputy spoke with such passion and creativity about the new role that they decided immediately that she should have it instead.

Here was my clue. At our next meeting, I suggested that we set the past aside and start to explore her options for the future. I think she was so exhausted by grief that she agreed without thinking. Perhaps it was a relief to talk about something else. Perhaps she had finally given up on her hopes. For whatever reason, she began hesitantly to tell me about her values and what she really longed for in her work. At the eleventh hour, she was able to change her attitude to what had happened and make a momentous choice: to let go of the past and look into a future she felt was bleak and hopeless, seeking out options she was sure did not exist.

But options did exist. We began to explore different ways in which she could contribute and make a difference. We talked about her love of teaching younger nurses, and the stress she had been under in dealing with all the bureaucracy of her job. We explored her ability to take risks, and she recognized that her husband's unflinching support would still be there, even if she tried something new and made a mess of it. It took several weeks until her confidence returned and she started to explore new options actively and even enthusiastically.

In response to a government initiative to deal with a shortage of nurses, the local authorities throughout the region announced that they were establishing a new nurse training facility. It was to be larger, more modern and more closely linked to the region's hospitals than anything that had existed before. The first step in the process was to choose the person to head up the project.

Now my client was excited, truly excited. She talked about the role with passion and enthusiasm, ideas tumbling over themselves as she saw all the possibilities. She applied. She went — nervously — to the interviews. She was appointed to the position. It was better paid, more prestigious and far more suited to expanding her potential than the role she had lost. Sometimes there are happy endings, even in real life.

Missing the momentous choices

During our lifetime, we make hundreds of thousands of choices. Few are really important, but every now and then one turns out to be crucial and life changing. Because we typically choose through habit, most of these decisions are over so quickly that we barely register them. The automatic pilot cuts in and the decision is made and acted upon in a flash. If we agonize, it is often *after* the decision has been made, wondering if we got it right. That is why we nearly always miss the life changing opportunities. They get mixed in with the rest and are gone before we notice what is happening. We are missing out on our own lives. When something wakes us up, it is no wonder we do not know how we came to be where we are. But when we are truly committed to something, the universe has an odd way of suddenly opening doors that we never noticed were there.

Conscious choice is the *only* way to realize potential. There is no other route. Viktor Frankl, whose words head this chapter, was an Austrian psychiatrist and a Jew. When the Nazis came, neither were healthy attributes. He spent the war in concentration camps, struggling to survive like everyone else. He could have been forgiven for fixing his attention on nothing more than making it to the next day. But he was blessed by the kind of curiosity that all great thinkers display, so he tried to make sense of the horrors around him. That was where he started to discover the untold power of conscious choice — a power that even the most sadistic Nazi bullies could not take away. In our different lives, you and I must also use conscious choice to realize our potential — it is the only process that is strong enough to break through our years of habit and conditioning. It is the only thing that *works*.

This is a vital point, so I am going to take it slowly and in sequence. If you are keen to move ahead, you can skip the next few paragraphs.

We have already established what we must change if we want to connect with our untapped potential. Learning needs fresh experiences as fuel and we must provide them. This means stepping outside our comfort zone and trying new options.

To be able to learn from what happens, we must also know what we are doing and *why*. We can compare our intentions and actions to the results we obtain, always allowing for the general perversity of things and the operations of chance. Potential is made of possibilities drawn from all the things we do *not* do at present. This deliberate process of choosing to do things differently will therefore ensure that we are constantly having to do things we do not do now — and that means constant opportunities for accessing more of our potential. Because we are doing this consciously, we can be attentive to see how it works out. Trying new things and seeing what happens is the basis for all true learning.

As we continue this process, we will expand our experience, our knowledge and, most likely, our skill. We will find new things, and see old things in new ways. We will come across fresh options and ideas. All this will increase our understanding. We will become different people — less bound by the past, more open to the future. Because human beings remember what they do, and generalize specific experiences into larger rules and concepts, we will also add to our ability to cope with situations and events that we cannot yet see or even imagine. We will grow and access more of our potential, and thus be better able to deal effectively with new situations as they arise.

What is the essential process that makes all this possible? *It is simply the repeated decision to replace automatic, habitual actions and thoughts with conscious choice.*

WE ALL FIND ourselves accessing unrealized potential from time to time, whether we like it or not. Life's problems and traumas see to that. We have already seen that people display amazing talents under the stress of a disaster. But that is not a mode of learning that is ever likely to be popular. We can be certain that the people who suggest that we will learn best by being thrown in at the deep end are the ones who will stay safe and dry on the bank, watching us try not to drown. Even if we make it to the shore, we will not have learned how to swim. Those who access untapped talent under stress rarely have much energy left over to note how they are doing what they do, so it is unlikely they will learn how do it again. They have *experienced* something of their unutilized potential, but they have not learned how to access it *deliberately*.

A SPARK FROM HEAVEN?

You cannot claim to have learned something until you can recall it whenever you want. The same is true of potential. You only fully realize potential when you can use it whenever you desire. Like scientists — and we should all aspire to be scientists in the study of our own lives — we must not accept single experiences as facts, unless they can be verified by being repeated on demand.

Scientists have developed a process — the scientific method — that allows them to learn deliberately. Since we are used to it being around, we no longer notice how amazing it is. For thousands of years, people tried to discover things about this world without such a process. Such revered thinkers as Plato, Aristotle and Pythagoras had little or no notion of the power of conducting experiments. They thought about things, and invented much of the logical basis for modern science, but they never carried out deliberate experiments to test their ideas. Yet once the scientific method was invented, no one had to rely on chance observation or inspired guesses anymore. They could experiment and see for themselves.

Experimentation is the heart of the scientific method. You establish an expectation that something specific will happen as a result of what you are going to do — that is the hypothesis — then test this hypothesis by conducting the experiment, guarding carefully against chance results. If you get the outcome you expect, you try it again, probably many times. When you are convinced the experiment can be replicated at will, you publish your results and other scientists also try to repeat them. If they succeed, your hypothesis becomes an accepted theory; and if it stands the test of time without suddenly producing unexpected outcomes, it gets dignified with the title of a law of nature.

Newton's law of gravity depends on the observable fact that every single apple falls to the ground, however often you try it.

This is exactly the process we need to follow to access our potential deliberately. First, we establish a hypothesis, substituting a conscious choice for an unconscious habit. It is no use doing things at random. Random results cannot be traced back to a specific cause, so you cannot repeat them. You have to choose consciously and deliberately, doing something that is different than your usual behavior in similar circumstances, and with the clear intention of producing a different, but *expected* result.

Let us take an example. Suppose that you are the kind of person who finds it tough to make snap decisions. You see an opportunity, but hesitate to take action without careful thought. Sometimes this saves you from rash actions, so it feels good. Just as often, it prevents you from taking the kind of risks that lead to breakthroughs in your performance, or innovation in your thinking. You have always *seen* what you might do, but rarely acted on what you saw. In seeking safety, you know you have lost the fun of life.

Now another opportunity comes up. The old habits cut in, but this time you decide, quite deliberately and coolly, to spend no more than a few moments looking at the options carefully and consciously. What is the real risk of failure? What would you lose by taking a risk? Would it really matter if things did not turn out as you hoped? Could you survive a small loss of face?

You decide to seize the opportunity and *consciously* accept the risks. Whether the outcome of this experiment works as you anticipate or not, you have set the basis for learning. You know *what* you did and *why* you did it. You know what resulted. With some care and repeated experimentation, you can decipher the link between decisions and results.

Let us assume you took the risk and it failed. Okay, it did not produce what you wanted. But because you know *what* you did and *why*, you can work out at least some of the reasons for failure. Perhaps you lacked some area of skill. Perhaps you moved too quickly or too slowly. Perhaps you were still too tentative.

Armed with this knowledge, you can try again. Maybe you get a better result. What worked that did not work before? The more that you can understand these causal links between deliberate actions and their results, the more often you will be able to produce the right outcome — always allowing for chance events and the unpredictability of the universe. You have learned something that has increased your ability and added to your confidence. You have realized another small piece of your potential *permanently*.

Whenever we behave automatically and without conscious thought, the process of cause and effect is hidden from us. It is there, of course. But since we are not conscious of why we did what we did — let alone the circumstances in which we did it — there is no possible way of learning from the result. We know what we intended, but when it does not turn out as we expected, all we can do is wonder. Good, bad or indifferent, what happens simply happens, and we cannot tell how or why or whether it will happen that way again. Without conscious choice, there cannot be any learning. Without learning — deliberate learning — we cannot access unused potential by any mechanism other than chance.

Summary

* The interaction of our choices with the sum of events around us produces our future. Choice is the ultimate human freedom, but our automatic habits usually block it.
* Every choice is a priceless opportunity to seek out new possibilities and realize more potential. Even the most mundane choices may conceal options that can change our lives.
* If we allow our habits to rule our lives, we will miss crucial experiences.
* To be able to learn from our experience, we must always know what we are doing and why. By doing this consciously, we can trace the patterns of cause and effect. Doing this deliberately allows us to repeat what we learn at any time.

FOURTEEN

CONCEPTS AND TOOLKITS

> Nothing is more dangerous than an idea if it's the only one you have.
>
> ALAIN

> Every real thought on every real subject knocks the wind out of somebody or other.
>
> OLIVER WENDELL HOLMES

> It isn't what people think that is important, but the reason they think what they think.
>
> ICNESCO

A concept is a piece of learning that has been generalized so it can be applied in many different contexts. Our memories are not good at holding the details of thousands of different events, but they are superb at keeping and recalling concepts. Many animals learn, but only humans can turn what they learn into concepts. Forming concepts is essential to accessing potential. The more concepts we develop about how to find ways out of problems, or turn events to our advantage, the more skillfully we can deal with whatever turns up.

Concepts are like wrench sets. If you have too small a set, you can be sure that you will never have the one you need when the lawn tractor breaks down. Smart people buy huge wrench sets containing every possible size, imperial and metric, just in case. Smart people also keep as many concepts as possible stored away in their memories. One of the factors that most observers rate as part of potential is this ability to step up to new or unpredicted situations and come out smiling.

A successful concept is the mental equivalent of a law of nature. It is something that you have tried many times in widely varying contexts and it has always produced pretty much the expected outcome.

In talking with thousands of managers I have always noticed that those who seem least successful and most frustrated have the fewest available concepts. You can tell this because they keep using the same ones over and over again, regardless of how well these ideas fit. Like people whose Christmas present was a socket set with only five sockets, they have few choices. If their sockets do not fit, they do the best they can, even if that means stripping the head off the bolt.

In direct contrast, discussing some challenging topic with a person who has been successful in filling a number of senior positions often results in an amazing display of the ability to create and recall concepts. It is not a universal law. Some people get to the top by other means, and a few do not deserve to be there, yet more often than not the thing you notice first about highly successful people is the wealth of mental concepts they have at their beck and call.

Attention! Attention!

There is plenty of evidence that human minds only have a limited amount of attention available at any time. People forced to divide their attention across several simultaneous tasks experience a drop in performance on *everything* they are doing.

Potential begins with the conscious choice to take charge of our attention and focus on what matters. We only have so much attention available, so if we allow multiple thoughts, fears or imaginings to monopolize it, there is not enough left over for making conscious choices.

Whenever we are under pressure or feel uncertain and confused, we go right back to operating from habit. It is as if our minds can only handle so much before they have to gain a respite by switching on the autopilot and taking a little nap. It is little wonder that we often arrive somewhere we do not want to be. If we keep repeating the process, blaming everything except the most likely cause — our own automatic behavior — we will stay trapped and confused.

It has become fashionable to boast about the ability to multi-task. You regularly see people trying to do several complex activities at the same time. Perhaps they truly believe that it is possible to divide attention into parts while each part remains unaffected. Of course, this is nonsense. When attention is fragmented, performance falls. That has been proved in the laboratory as well as in daily life. We never have more than 100 percent of our attention available. Split it two ways and each task gets 50 percent, or one gets 75 percent and the other only 25 percent.

Once we have used up 100 percent of our attention there is *nothing left over*. We may try to fool ourselves into believing that we can multi-task and somehow increase our attention to match. It is not so. People who try to focus on several things simultaneously are able to give only limited attention to each one. Our attention is finite. Period.

WHAT WE FOCUS on expands. This is also the nature of attention. Whatever we pay attention to powerfully and consistently will always grow larger in our lives. We all know this, but our exposure to it is often negative. Remember when you last had a really serious problem to worry about? Remember how it spawned all kinds of off-shoots and fresh anxieties? How it claimed all your attention and grew to dominate your thinking until it was resolved? The good news is that what happens in this negative sense also happens in a positive one. If you also recall a time when you were fully caught up in some pleasurable activity, you will know from your own experience what it is like to have no attention to spare for anything else.

If we pay close attention knowingly and deliberately to realizing our potential, it will expand in our lives until we are able to produce extraordinary results. By giving most of our attention to actions which will increase potential, we will also find there will not be much left over for worry or depression. If we starve our fearful imaginings and daydreaming of attention, they will wither away.

This is the process followed by every Olympic athlete, every top performer, and every outstanding achiever in any fields of human endeavor. Outside their chosen area, they are ordinary people. What is not ordinary is the tightly focused attention they bring, consciously and purposely, to whatever aspect of their potential they want to accomplish.

The strengths we pay attention to *always* expand. Whatever we ignore *always* diminishes. So if we have a talent or strength and concentrate our attention on it, it will grow stronger. If we take it for granted, it will fade away. Athletes practice, opera singers rehearse, and football stars train every day so that their strengths do not fail when they need them. They focus their attention repeatedly on what they want to perfect. You cannot learn if your attention is elsewhere. That is another trick your habits play on you. By convincing you that you can give your attention to other things while they run the show, they will slowly deprive you of the strengths you already have, as well as stopping you from developing new ones.

Conscious choice allows us to bring *all* our attention to our decisions, so we can learn from the consequences. Of course, it is much slower than automatic behavior. The speed of habitual reactions makes them seductive in a culture that values action over reflection. Just remember that it is the same speed that may carry us past an important decision so that we are barely aware of making it at all.

An imaginary world of scarcity

If you had the choice, would you rather live in a world of scarcity or one of abundance? This is not a silly question. We have this choice every day, but mostly we choose to live in the world of scarcity. We have made that irrational choice so often that we have come to believe that there is no other world. Scarcity is what we accept as normal.

In a world of scarcity, there is never enough of anything to go round. It is a zero-sum world: for me to have some opportunity or benefit, you must lose out by the same amount. For John or Mary to win promotions, Ellen or Michael must be set aside. We are easily convinced that scarcity is how things are. It must be true that promotions, or pay raises, or even interesting jobs are limited in number. If two or three people want the same role, only one of them can have it. Money for pay raises is finite. In an attempt to give some mathematical basis for distribution, many organizations resort to approaches that force payments into a set distribution. Only 10 percent of people can have this much; only 30 percent the next largest amount.

It is easy for us to assume that this is true of everything in our lives. When we set our hearts on some goal and it eludes us, we assume that it was not our turn: that someone else won the prize, so we could not have it as well. If we find ourselves losing out more often than we wish, we begin to suspect that the system is somehow biased against us. Someone is fiddling the odds.

YET THERE IS no logical reason for us to assume that intangible things like joy, excitement, stimulation and fulfillment are also subject to some form of cosmic rationing. If I have an exciting and fulfilling life, it does not follow that you must forego a similar opportunity. We assume scarcity only because we choose to do so. Perhaps as children we heard some adult telling us that few people could expect an enjoyable life. People like us had to make do with the scraps. Perhaps some time when we were disap-

A SPARK FROM HEAVEN?

pointed and upset, someone tried to comfort us with the idea that our turn would come.

The view of the world as a place of constant scarcity is all around us. People try to use it to feel better about their lives. They insist that somewhere all the good things that *they* ought to have are being enjoyed by the rich, or idle, or scheming, or white, or male, or young, or whatever other category of human beings they assume to be privileged. What should have been theirs has been taken from them unfairly, and there is nothing they can do about it.

The inevitable result of this thinking is cynicism and alienation. If we choose to inhabit a world where material scarcities are assumed to indicate scarcities in non-material benefits, we will become frustrated and bitter. Instead of attempting to question this belief, we settle into the attitude that it is all we can expect.

Sadly, cynicism about potential is widespread. Many people assume that they are too old, too poor, too uneducated, too honest, or too far gone to aspire to happiness or satisfaction at work. That is for other people: the ones who seem to possess all the attributes that they lack. Cynicism is seductive precisely because it contains a strong element of truth. Maybe others do seem to have what we lack. The question is *"why?"*

IF WE ASSUME that positive emotions and outcomes such as satisfaction or fulfillment are severely rationed, the best we can do is to be content with what we have. Yet it is not a matter of *having* at all. We cannot *possess* satisfaction or joy. We can only *be* satisfied and joyful. And if I am joyful, what prevents you from being joyful as well, and hundreds of thousands — even billions — of other people too?

Life is sometimes unpleasant. We get hurt. We have our hopes dashed. We fail. That is how it is. Suffering is not rationed. There is plenty of it to go around, and then some. And fulfillment is not rationed either. It is also abundant. If we choose to cultivate a cynical outlook, and deny ourselves the possibility of satisfactory lives, that is our choice. When it becomes habitual, we will surely get what we chose.

Those who choose to understand that no one needs to lose for them to win will still suffer setbacks and pain. Yet their attitude can be that they always have another chance. They can pick themselves up, dust themselves off, and start all over again. Perhaps next time it will work out, or the time after that.

Potential is possibility and possibility has no limits. It is *never* in scarce supply. We do not have to assume we are victims. We *choose* to do this. We do not have to be cynical. We *choose* to be. We can withhold our commitment to life and growth, and demand proof and certainty as the price for making an investment in our own future. If we do that, we will never move from where we are. If the outcome was certain, there would be no call for commitment.

We must always remember that choice produces consequences. Realizing potential is a choice that requires an act of faith, based on commitment to our own future and the belief that a more satisfactory and skillful life is possible. *No absolute proof of this is available.* There is no certainty of the outcome. Outcomes in real life are never assured.

In 1921, Frank Knight, professor of Economics at the University of Chicago, pointed out the true difference between risk and uncertainty[10]. Risk is randomness, he said, but its probabilities can be determined. In economics, risky situations do not usually produce profitable opportunities, because anyone can calculate the odds and take the same chance. Uncertainty implies the probabilities are unknown or unknowable. *Only uncertain change creates profitable situations.*

When the future outcome is not known, the likelihood of success is unique, however many people join the game. One person may scoop the jackpot, or the jackpot itself may turn out to be so large that scores of groups can all make enormous profits, and there will still be wealth left over. What is true of business economics is true of our working lives. Uncertainty is full of possibilities — the raw stuff of potential. Risk is simply a matter of finite odds.

Building your toolkit

Slow down. Quick responses almost always originate in automatic habits. Let us work through an example. Suppose Lucy's boss asks her to take on a demanding project that she knows she is not really qualified to handle. She could immediately say no. However, she is working on realizing more of her potential, so she asks to think it over for a while. She asks herself — and also her boss — why the organization has offered her this job. Do they see something in her that she does not see in herself? If she takes it on, what will she lose? As well as looking at the risk (the odds), she carefully includes the element of uncertainty as well and all the possibilities that offers. The odds them-

---

[10] See Select Bibliography under Frank Hyneman Knight, 1921.

selves are uncertain. Maybe she could find talents in her self she has been ignoring? She takes her time to think it through. Her decision may still be incorrect, but she will know why she made it. Whatever happens, she now has the basis for learning. If she takes the job, win or fail she can match the outcome to her choice. If she stands aside, she can reflect later on how that decision played out.

We often fail to take enough time to avoid thoughtless reactions, or to be fully conscious of what we are doing. Habitual responses are easy. When we are rushed, hassled and stressed, we feel there is neither time nor energy to spend on making things more complex or difficult. So we limit our options to those that appear habitually and stay in our comfort zone, choosing between possibilities we have seen many times before. It is all so familiar, so secure and predictable. No wonder we sleepwalk through our working lives.

Conscious choices feel less comfortable and demand more mental energy than automatic ones, but they also offer unique opportunities to learn. Because of this, conscious choice is never worthless. Win or lose, we will learn something useful.

AFTER WE HAVE slowed down, we must make sure we look at *as many options as we can discover*, not just those that appear automatically. Lucy does this. She ponders some important questions. Is this an opportunity to make a big stretch and realize a great deal of potential at one time? What would be the *real* risk of the project not being a success? Would her life end? Would her career? What would she learn by taking on this project? What would she gain if she succeeded?

It is a mistake to narrow our focus and restrict our choices. The narrower the range of options we consider, the greater the chance that we will miss an opportunity to connect with some piece of potential. Narrow-minded people get that way because they habitually think and act in narrow ways. Broadening our outlook and finding new perspectives is one of the best and simplest ways to increase access to our potential. *Open your mind and welcome uncertainty. It is full of opportunities.*

It is worth a brief digression to look at the difference between being narrow-minded and being focused. To be focused, we need first to make a choice. We look at the options, decide on the one or two that appear most promising, then focus on those, ignoring all distractions. Being narrow-minded means never having to say we are doubtful. The blinders we put on ourselves restrict our view to one dimension. What is not white is black. With tunnel vision, it is easy to mistake the light ahead for the end of the tunnel, when it is really an approaching train.

TAKING CHARGE of our attention is the third essential step along the way to realizing potential. When we direct our attention consciously and deliberately, we can focus it where it is most beneficial.

Many people's habitual action is to focus most of their attention on the risks. We are such fearful creatures. One whiff of trouble and we let our minds run wild, imagining all kinds of pessimistic and fearful outcomes. We conjure up so many demons that we become distracted and stressed. Why not try looking carefully at one option at a time? Follow it through and see where it leads. Then take another option and do the same, directing attention where it should go. If we do not let our fears and worries make us confused, we will stay focused on the possibilities and avoid anxiety and stress.

Remember that whatever we give full attention to expands. Since that often means withdrawing our attention for a while from less important matters, it may not be an easy decision. Some of the people around us — especially our bosses — demand attention exactly when they want it, regardless of just about everything else! Like so much else in our lives, we rarely have complete control over what we do. But that does not mean we have *no* control. However put upon we may feel, we can still take charge of our attention consciously whenever we can. If we want to make a conscious choice, we must give it sufficient attention. Habitual and automatic choices demand no attention at all.

LET US RETURN to Lucy and the project her boss wants her to take on. She has slowed down, broadened her perspective, looked carefully at the options and directed her attention. Now she faces the fourth step: making the decision.

She tries to stand back and see this prospect in the context of her work and career as a whole. Calmly and without fearfulness, she considers the risks of failure and the chances of success. Like most people when they deal with reality instead of imagination, she quickly realizes that failure is not going to bring her career or her life to an end, however much her anxiety is telling her it will. About the worst that can happen is that she will lose face and a few mean spirited folk will laugh. So she goes back to her boss and gives her honest view of the possibilities, sharing her perspective on the options and explaining how she has weighed the outcomes. Whether she finally says yes or no, she has already learned something new — and probably increased her boss's respect for her calmness and thoughtfulness.

There is no sure-fire way of getting it right every time. Some decisions are simply too difficult, or too obscure, or too emotionally draining. That is how life is. We often foul up. Just the same, exercising conscious choice is *always* beneficial, even when the decision proves to be a real bummer.

Responses versus reactions

Even mistakes work to our long-term advantage when we use conscious choice. Because we chose deliberately and with full attention, we see clearly why we acted as we did. Comparing the reasoning to the result lets us learn from our successes *and* our failures. Automatic choices would deny us that chance.

CONSCIOUS CHOICE also allows us to step past our automatic habits and look at more options. Doing this carefully increases our chances for success. It also lets us get to work on dismantling obsolete or inappropriate habits and strengthening successful ones, until outworn patterns no longer function. We learn to *respond*, not just react.

Reacting is spontaneous and automatic. Responding implies taking time to choose an appropriate reply, and creates the space to produce a more effective approach than the automatic reaction. It allows time for conscious choices. It makes available wider options and extra possibilities. It provides unlimited opportunities to learn and broaden our minds. This *always* allows more of our potential to be realized.

Why not decide *now* to stop relying on habitual, conditioned responses? Look carefully at every choice and action, exploring the options and possibilities that you usually ignore. Discover whatever is limiting you and step over it. As soon as you stretch beyond your comfort zone, you will add to your ability to respond more effectively in the future. Each small step outside realizes another piece of potential. *It is the only way.*

It is high time to change the habitual patterns of thinking that limit our perceptions. These patterns are well established and tough. They have been around nearly as long as we have — perhaps longer, if we have taken some of them from our parents, our community or our culture. Our habits are so much part of us that we no longer recognize them as patterns we can *choose to set aside*. Our habits have taken over our minds and we need to take them back.

Summary

- What happens to us in our future depends in large part on the choices we make today. Either we make those choices consciously, or our automatic habits will make them for us.
- Every choice is an opportunity to realize more of our potential. We do not know in advance which choice may turn out to be momentous. If we remain conscious, we will not miss it.
- Only conscious choice is strong enough to break through habits. By making deliberate decisions, we can track the results and relate cause to effect.

A SPARK FROM HEAVEN?

- Smart, successful people generalize their learning into concepts that can be applied to many situations.
- How we allocate our attention is crucial. Attention enhances whatever it is applied to, positive or negative. If we give our strengths attention, they will grow. If we starve our gifts of attention, they will diminish.
- Intangible things like joy, success, stimulation and fulfillment are not in limited supply. Potential is possibility and possibility is limitless.
- Realizing potential is an act of faith and commitment. Uncertainty is our friend, providing new opportunities for profitable changes.
- We can all practice increasing conscious choice, using these guidelines:
  - Take your time.
  - Explore more options than you would automatically consider.
  - Direct your attention deliberately. Do not let your habits do it for you.
  - Trust yourself and accept that sometimes you will get it wrong.
  - Try to respond consciously to events instead of simply reacting to them automatically.

FIFTEEN

CONSCIOUS INCOMPETENCE

> "Far better it is to dare mighty things, to win glorious triumphs even though checkered by failure, than to rank with those poor spirits who neither enjoy nor suffer much because they live in the gray twilight that knows neither victory nor defeat."
>
> — THEODORE ROOSEVELT

> "Success is the ability to go from one failure to another with no loss of enthusiasm."
>
> — SIR WINSTON CHURCHILL

If a thing is worth doing, it is worth doing badly! If something is truly important to you — like becoming the person you know you have it in you to be — it is *really* worth doing badly. Forget all about doing it right the first time. This is not a book about quality assurance. It is a book about how to explore and connect with your potential. *In the real world, doing something new almost always means doing it badly the first time.*

I would like to introduce you to the tremendous power of *conscious incompetence*. Once you have discovered where your potential is, you must be willing to start realizing it — and that means doing things you know you are going to do *very badly*. It may be fun to read about the guy who wrestled a shark to retrieve a child's arm that it had bitten off, or how Bill Gates rose from obscurity to be the richest man in the world. That is motivational, but it will not tell *you* how to get more access to *your* potential in *your* life.

New events and new situations are the essentials for learning; and learning is the only route I know for accessing potential. That means doing lots of things for the first time. What is it like when you do something you have not done before? *You do a pretty poor job.* You do it *badly*. There is no other way to learn. If you are only willing to do things well, you cannot do anything new. To develop your potential you must start to cultivate a new skill: the skill of *conscious incompetence*.

For an organization, a team or John Doe, accessing fresh potential means learning — and learning means starting out by doing things imperfectly. *Accessing potential consciously and deliberately means doing things badly on purpose, so you can learn to do them well.* That is what is meant by conscious incompetence. To access more potential, we begin by deliberately stepping outside our comfort zone and doing things we know we cannot yet do competently. We understand fully what is going to happen and we do it just the same.

The need to recognize conscious incompetence is so obvious that in almost any other context it would not be worth mentioning. In the world of work, however, there is so much pressure for doing things correctly from the start that people live in a constant state of anxiety. If we are not allowed a period of grace to learn by doing things badly, we had better stick to what we know we can do. If we are to "hit the ground running" in a business that has "no room for passengers," we must either do everything competently from the start or risk being pushed aside as a liability.

The result of such needless torment is that people draw back from new areas. They have survived to the point of doing something capably, so they do not want to risk themselves by stepping outside this hard-won comfort zone. They do only what they have done before. Habit — the sworn enemy of potential — is running their lives.

DEFENSIVE HABITS come in many forms. Take the tough guys who run certain large operations. They have developed defensive habits of management that put cost cutting and quarterly results at the top of their agendas. They "squeeze the fat out of the operation" and "run a tight ship." Since Wall Street has its own defensive habit of mindlessly applauding this kind of behavior, mostly because it boosts apparent short-term profits, the tough guys think what they are doing is clever stuff and their short-sighted habits are reinforced. They never notice that they are also removing the ability to grow and learn — which is why many organizations managed by people like this seem to exist in a constant state of crisis, despite all the "tough measures" and "cost cutting scenarios" they inflict on themselves. Reactive and defensive short-term gain quickly produces long-term pain.

Practicing conscious incompetence

Conscious incompetence should be required behavior in every organization. It is the only way for people to access their untapped potential *deliberately* and put it to use. This is true for individuals, teams and the whole organization. We all access bits and pieces of our potential by chance, whether we want to or not. The world makes demands on us that we cannot avoid, and those demands sometimes force us along new paths. Realizing potential is a perfectly natural activity. But only taking that activity and making it *deliberate* will allow us to realize our potential whenever and wherever and however we want.

How do you practice conscious incompetence? Carefully, for a start. We have to learn when to practice this vital skill of deliberately being incompetent, and when to leave it alone. If we do it all the time, people will believe we really are incompetent. We all have jobs to do that demand competent actions, so most of the time we have to provide what is needed and act competently.

The best time to practice conscious incompetence is when we are making decisions. Remember that our potential lies in the choices we make. Since conscious incompetence is the best way to develop potential, the best time and place to use it is where our potential hides: in our choices and decisions.

HERE IS HOW this works. Let us assume that Tom is the kind of person for whom the notion of incompetence is as welcome as the notion of intestinal parasites. Tom is faced with a decision. What does he do? He does not want to make a mistake, or take risks he can avoid. He believes the best way to meet both objectives is to use his memory and knowledge to see how this kind of decision has been made before and replicate it.

Since Tom is an intelligent guy who prides himself on being competent, he knows where to look for this information: in the past. He remembers what he has done before that turned out well. He recalls what he learned at business school and corporate training events. He searches out industry best practice. He learns *about* things he already knows, and uses this knowledge to make a decision that has the best chances of being correct *in terms of past knowledge*. Tom knows no one ever got fired for following industry best practice or buying IBM. He is a cautious person. That is why he will probably never develop more than a fraction of his potential.

Now Julia comes up against the same decision as Tom, but she decides it is a great chance for stealthily practicing conscious incompetence. Conscious incompetence is best done in secret. The rest of the world tends to misunderstand.

Julia does every thing that Tom does, but adds the magic ingredient that is going to transform her career. She takes time to review all the other options she can think up that do not match industry best practice, and are *not* in line with how things have been done before. She knows that she is not likely to be good at them, but she checks them out just the same. By doing this she has started adding to her understanding. She is learning things, not just learning *about* things.

Suppose she comes across an option that looks highly promising. The trouble is she does not know how to make it happen. It is not a safe choice, like Tom's, but it could be extremely successful for her and her company. Julia goes into learning overdrive. She researches the idea, learns a little bit about how to do it, puts it forward and gets it accepted. Once she has approval, she starts to implement her idea. She makes lots of mistakes — she knew she had no initial competence to help her — but each one teaches her more. She persists in the face of failure. By the end of the project, Julia has accessed another portion of her potential, the company has gained a new approach, and senior management has recognized a talent in the making. Tom is still polishing his existing knowledge, and wonders why his career is not progressing far.

Mentors as protectors

In an ideal world, every company would make space for conscious incompetence, and support people practicing it for the benefit of the organization. It is not an ideal world. That is why it is often better to practice this process in secret. The alternative is to find a powerful mentor. Senior people have always acted as mentors to younger talented folk, long before someone picked up the idea and tried to turn it into a technique to be applied like corporate whitewash. The most important gift these natural mentoring relationships gave to the junior member of the pairing was *protection*. Knowledge, wisdom and experience were shared as well, but protection was most important: protection to be able to practice conscious incompetence without fear of being caught and punished.

In about the fourth year of my working life, I was selected by a very senior person to be mentored. She was the head of the department in which I was working, and about seven rungs in the management hierarchy above me. Do not ask me why I was chosen. I was not a prepossessing choice. About the only distinguishing characteristic I had was arrogance.

Anyhow, she took me under her wing and I grabbed the chance with both hands. Just one example of what happened will show how I leapt at the opportunity to practice conscious incompetence and how she helped me do it safely. It happened one August in, I guess, 1972.

My job at that time was to handle recruitment into the managerial ranks of the organization. Had I been Tom, I would have looked at the way it had been done before, checked on how other leading organizations did it, and applied what I learned. I was not like Tom. With no competence in advanced recruitment techniques and no plan of action, I looked at what had been done in the past and decided I could do better. What I needed was the means of setting a strategy the organization would accept; one that would demand the changes in selection procedures I wanted to make. Armed with little more than a few notes and a lot of nerve, I went to see Mrs. Fox.

She listened, asked penetrating questions, then sent me away to work out the details. She never questioned why I had decided we needed to change processes that had been in place for a decade. She sent me back to my office to collect the proof. When I returned I had a plan. Unfortunately, the plan included the design of a computer-based succession-planning program to set the strategy. Computers in those days in England filled large rooms. I had never seen one, and had no idea how to write any kind of program.

Mrs. Fox listened again, asked me more questions, and told me she would think about what I had said. A week later she called me back to her office. I was provided with a computer programmer to work on my project full time, unlimited access to the company's mainframe during the night to run my software, and a pat on the head to send me on my way. I was barely twenty-five years old.

I ran the software, presented the results, and was allowed almost a free hand to transform the recruitment process. What resulted was far better than before, despite my inexperience. For the first time we had a system designed expressly for our needs, not one handed down from others in the industry. We also had an up-to-date system. It won me a promotion.

There is a sequel to this story that shows what happens when the enemy — habit — takes over. More than fifteen years after the events of that August, I had moved to another company, and forgotten all about my youthful exploits in computerized human resource planning. I met someone at a conference and we got talking about our respective careers. To our surprise, we found that we had both worked in that same organization I was a part of in 1972. He had joined a few years after I had left.

"Did they have *The Program* in your day?" he asked me. I expressed surprise. "What program?" He explained that in his time in the organization, there existed a computer program that determined every aspect of the way people were recruited, trained and deployed. Its output was obeyed without question, though no one quite understood how it had come into being, or why it was followed so slavishly.

"It was a monster," he told me. "No one understood it, but no one was prepared to risk turning it off either or taking any different decisions."

To my shame, I shook my head and told him that I had never come across such a thing. "It must," I said quickly, "have been put in place after I left."

Summary

* Accessing potential consciously and deliberately means doing things badly *on purpose*, so that you can learn to do them well. That is what is meant by conscious incompetence.
* New events and new situations are the essentials for learning, which is the only route to accessing potential. That means doing lots of things for the first time and probably doing them badly. If you are only willing to do things well, you cannot do anything new.
* To access more potential, we must begin by deliberately stepping outside our comfort zones and doing things we know we cannot yet do competently.
* The best time to practice conscious incompetence is when we are making decisions. Conscious incompetence is also best done in secret. The alternative is to find a powerful mentor.
* Conscious incompetence should be required behavior in every organization. It is the only way for people to access their untapped potential deliberately and put it to use.

SIXTEEN

THE EVEN BIGGER PICTURE

> Nothing in life is to be feared. It is only to be understood.
>
> MARIE CURIE

> A pile of rocks ceases to be a rock pile when somebody contemplates it with the idea of a cathedral in mind.
>
> ANTOINE DE SAINT-EXUPÉRY

We are often urged to look at the Big Picture when a difficult decision is in front of us. This is good advice. Standing back and putting something into a broader context often helps us to see it more clearly. It can also reveal solutions that escaped us before.

There is a natural process in human beings that seeks to give *meaning* to everything that occurs in our lives. It is as if we cannot feel comfortable unless we understand why things happen and what they mean. Events that seem meaningless upset us and cause us to experience some degree of dislocation. Viktor Frankl wrote about a "will to meaning," an innate process in all of us that seeks to give some meaning to our existence and the things that happen to us[11]. People who lack this sense are often depressed and negative about themselves and those around them. In some cases, having a well-developed sense that life has some meaning is viewed as one of the criteria of mental health.

We can more or less prove this for ourselves by watching and listening. How often do we hear others — or ourselves — commenting on events about which we have little or no knowledge? How many of those comments are based on explaining what the event really means, and why or how it is significant? The media are full of just this kind of reporting. Whatever happens must be explained, at least to the satisfaction of the journalist or commentator. And if no explanation presents itself, one is quickly assumed, or imagined, or sometimes invented. But have you ever stopped to ask why this technique works? What is the process that enables us to see different aspects of any issue, merely by shifting where we are standing mentally?

Meaning changes with *context*. In fact, meaning is given by context in most situations. The context in which words are spoken, or events take place, determines how we interpret them. The meaning they have for us arises from the situation in which we encounter them.

LET US TAKE a simple example. Suppose that I find a note on my desk that reads: "I need you. Please come as soon as you can. Bring what we talked about earlier." The

---

[11] See Select Bibliography under Viktor E. Frankl, 1978.

surface meaning seems quite clear: someone needs me to go to him or her, taking whatever we had discussed when the two of us spoke last.

If the note is signed by my boss, I could be excited or apprehensive. Which feeling will come to me depends on the context of my relationship with my superior. If it is good, I may assume that my boss values my help, and this will provide an opportunity for me to take on some exciting and perhaps challenging work. If my boss and I are not on good terms, I may immediately assume that I am in some kind of trouble and will quickly start reviewing what I have done to cause this urgent summons. Of course, if I recall what we discussed earlier, I have a strong clue. If it was my suggestion for important changes to some key aspect of my work, I might conclude that I am to be given the go-ahead to proceed. If it was my annual performance appraisal, my level of apprehension might soar! If I cannot recall what is being referred to in the note, I might also feel rather worried.

But suppose the signature on the note is from a good friend. Now I may assume that he or she is in some kind of trouble. Perhaps we talked earlier about the rumor that some people might lose their jobs and I mentioned that I had the address of a good career counselor. Armed with that context, the meaning of the note becomes quite apparent: my friend has been let go and needs my help and comfort.

To complete the triad of possible contexts, let us suppose that the note is signed by a simple initial. It is from my new girlfriend, and I recall that we talked only last evening about a present I had promised to buy her today. The meaning is obvious and I can hardly wait for work to end so I can rush to her. In the meantime, I exercise my mind with some pleasurable fantasies about what will happen when I get there. Little more work gets done that day!

Nothing has changed in the basic situation that I described. The words on the note are the same, but their meaning ranges from being ominous to suggesting something highly exciting and interesting. What changed in each case is the context. This shifting of context is the basis for most jokes and humor. We listen to something and assume it is in one context, but when the comedian gets to the punch line, the context suddenly changes and the ridiculous nature of the whole idea causes us to laugh. Satirists do the same trick: they present well known personalities in strange and far-fetched contexts, so that their personal foibles and peculiarities are given amusing or sometimes threatening twists. We see them in a different light, no longer admirable but stupid, greedy, vain or plain unpleasant.

This is the secret of the Big Picture. By changing the context for our experience from our narrow, immediate and local concerns to something much more long-term and inclusive of others, we see events in a new light. Our interpretation of their significance and their meaning changes as well. They signify something quite different.

Multiple contexts

We have already seen that there can be several different contexts operating in our lives at the micro level. The same is true at the level of the Big Picture. There can be more than one Big Picture context: perhaps the Big Picture at work, one at home and one that relates to the community in which we live. However, because the Big Picture works on a much larger scale that our normal perspective, the number of variant contexts tends to be smaller. We can only have a few Big Pictures before they begin to overlap so much that they merge into something still more comprehensive: the *Even Bigger Picture*.

IN PERSONAL TERMS, we may define the *Even Bigger Picture* as the context that encompasses our life and experience as a whole. It represents our place in the world. For organizations, each Big Picture is usually associated with some aspect of overall strategy. The *Even Bigger Picture* covers how the organization fits into the total scheme of things: the industry, current economic conditions, and the whole social and political environment. Once again, we can see it as the organization's place in its particular world.

Like the Russian dolls that nest one inside the next, our experience takes place in a series of ever larger contexts. At the smallest scale, we are engaged in a minute-by-minute series of events. At the largest, we may have some sense of our life as a whole, and its relationship to everything we encounter, at least as far as we can grasp it. People often attach words like *spiritual* or *transformational* to this sense of some overarching context that includes us and all the people we deal with. Others speak of the *interconnectedness* of everything that mystics and great religious leaders have been able to grasp in all its majesty. I am not sure that such high-flown ways of expressing the idea are helpful. They suggest either that it is rare and wonderful, or that we must have some suitable religious belief and training to grasp it. Neither is correct. What we need is simply the willingness to keep shifting the size and scale of context wider and wider, until we can go no further. When we reach the point where we cannot conceive of any greater scale for our understanding, we have arrived at the *Even Bigger Picture*. It is a natural and universal ability.

THIS ABILITY needs to be recognized and developed before it can become useful. If our habit is to deny the existence of any context wider than our immediate wishes and concerns, that narrowness of outlook will color everything we do, say or think. We will put blinders on ourselves and limit our viewpoint to the next few steps ahead.

Similarly, if we assume that the only wider contexts that exist are formed from the malevolence of others, the unfairness of the system, or our own helplessness because of some past trauma, we will remain trapped in negative and threatening worlds that we have ourselves created and continue to sustain. Breaking out of our "normal" context is essential if we are to see whether we have been putting ourselves in some kind of prison.

We can assume that fishes that live their whole lives in the water of a lake have no conception of the wider world that includes both their lake, the land around it (which they may sometimes glimpse), and all the rest of the world. In the same way, our grasp of the possibilities of our potential will be severely constrained if we have no inkling that there is a wider world than the little pond we inhabit on a minute-by-minute basis.

Creating perspective

In our studies over the years, we have found one pattern that recurs with great consistency: those who reach the most important and demanding positions in their working lives tend to operate much more of the time in wider contexts than those who remain in more humdrum positions. What is even more interesting is that this difference seems to be present long before either group reaches levels where it becomes obvious. You can find it in school children, young people in college and any group of recruits on their first day of work.

Some researchers have been so struck by this obvious difference in perspective that they have assumed it must be innate or formed so early in life that it might as well have been produced genetically. Unfortunately, they often go further and assert that it is unchanging. Their bleak message is that if you have not naturally developed the broad perspectives characteristic of many successful people, you never will. This is not correct. As we have seen, what keeps such mental processes stable in our lives is simply habit. We *can* widen our perspective, though breaking the habits that have held us in a set of self-inflicted blinders for many years may take a strong will, and months or even years of consistent effort.

Why should we bother? What will we gain by working to see events around us not just from the perspective of whatever Big Picture is available, but also from the viewpoint of the *Even Bigger Picture*?

Contexts and opportunities

When we shift our perspective, we see things differently. It is like walking around an object, looking at it from all angles. We see things we missed before that were not visible from our original viewpoint. Better still, every time we broaden our perspective, we gain access to wider, more inclusive options and greater possibilities. Possibility is the essence of potential, so taking a wider perspective gives us a way into unused and unrecognized potential. Of course, the *Even Bigger Picture* is the broadest perspective we can usually access at will, so it is the place where we can find most possibilities and learning options.

LET US SUPPOSE that I have a problem reaching my sales targets. I seem to be trying hard, but customers are wary and simply not buying as I expect them to do. From the narrow perspective of sales activities, I begin thinking about working harder on my calls, trying to get agreements to offer fresh discounts, or calling up reliable customers asking them to bring forward regular orders. Any of these may have some effect, but I am really clutching at straws, since I have little idea at this stage what the reason for the fall in expected sales may be. I am also using only methods that I have probably used many times before. They offer little or no chance for learning anything new.

Now let us imagine that I stand back and concentrate on the Big Picture: the strategy behind my daily efforts. From this vantage point I may understand that the organization's purpose at this stage in the business cycle is to find new customers and add to its customer base. That means that getting reliable customers to bring orders forward may help my sales figures for the month, but will have no effect on the wider strategy. In fact, I am mortgaging the future by this expedient, since those expedited orders will leave gaps later in the year that I cannot fill by the same means. Thinking about new customers not only inclines me more towards trying to get greater discounts, but indicates where any discounts should be used — purely for new customers and initial orders. Concentrating there seems most helpful. I might also look at how I am getting leads to potential new users, how up-to-date and attractive the marketing literature is, and whether there are any sources of customers I may be overlooking. The more I think about the wider issues, the more likely I am to spot fresh places or groups for prospecting, and more innovative ways of getting their attention. If I also act on these insights, I will learn something new and activate more of my unused potential.

By standing right back and looking through the perspective of the *Even Bigger Picture*, more insights will be found. Maybe I begin to think about how things look from the customer's point of view. Times are tough and they are all under pressure to cut costs. If I can present what I have in a way that shows how they can reduce their overall expenditure through my product or service, they will probably be more interested. We might also be able to look at payment terms that would have less impact on closely watched budgets. I might also realize that my approach has been less enthusiastic lately. I am feeling unhappy with my job and frustrated in my career goals. That is probably coming across to my customers in some way and causing them to feel uncertain about dealing with me. I have not been sleeping well and know I need a break to get my ideas straightened out and refresh my enthusiasm.

Taking a vacation when I am behind on sales does not seem immediately to be a good idea, but from the perspective of the *Even Bigger Picture* things look different. The more I think from that place, the more clearly I see that much of the problem with sales comes from my own feelings and lackluster behavior. Fixing that will be the best way to rectify the sales gap. Hammering away at customers, while becoming ever more depressed and frustrated myself, is not calculated to produce any useful results. It may well convince potential customers that they can write off my company long term, which would seriously hamper my efforts for months or years to come.

When economic times are hard, the temptation is to increase effort and slog away at poor results. From the perspective of the *Even Bigger Picture*, we might see that this is just another business cycle. We try to deal with the short-term gaps as best we can, but getting ready for the next upswing should be a much higher priority. The businesses that grasp fresh opportunities early in the cycle will be the ones who ride it to the top. In time, everyone else will get on the economic elevator; but it will probably run out of steam long before they are carried far from their starting point. The fate of the "dot com bubble" shows this clearly. The businesses that began the cycle usually survived, hurt but still operating. Those that jumped onto the bandwagon towards the middle and end of the cycle were the first to fall into bankruptcy.

Distinguishing causes from effects

Using the perspective of the *Even Bigger Picture* lets us distinguish much more clearly between causes and effects. In the sales example above, poor sales were the effect. By concentrating on them, we were missing the cause: the salesperson's lack of enthusiasm and interest due to career problems and fatigue. Until this cause was tackled, nothing else would produce much change. If an organization is suffering from poor economic conditions, or an unfavorable legislative climate, changing the payment structures or urging everyone to work harder will have little effect.

Confusion about causes (or symptoms) and the effects that bring them about is a primary reason for workplace problems. It is not a simple matter to get right. What appears to be a cause from one perspective (sales are poor *because* the sales force is not doing its job) may turn out to be only another effect when you broaden your viewpoint (our sales people cannot sell more *because* our products are more expensive and less effective than our competitors' offerings).

One of the curses of business is a tendency to seek simple answers to complicated issues. Like politicians, many business leaders want quick and simple answers that will win them the reputation of being magicians. When a magician pulls a rabbit out of an empty hat, or cuts an assistant in half, we know it is an illusion. When some high profile CEO conjures profits out of nowhere, we are asked to believe they are real. In Irish legend, leprechauns often gave unwary mortals a wish. The least wary would wish for great wealth and find themselves surrounded by bags of gold. But when daylight came, the gold coins in the bags usually turned into worthless golden leaves. The same thing happens to the profits. Most simple answers turn out in time to be illusions. Like the leprechaun, the magicians have usually departed rapidly before the trick becomes obvious.

The other current curse is trying to short circuit the need to think and explore by taking on a complete solution that appears to have worked elsewhere. So-called industry best practice is the organizational equivalent of the instant diet book, filled with pictures of people who have lost amazing amounts of weight without, it seems, making any effort. Millions of these books are sold every year, yet the population of most of the free world gets steadily more obese. The books are amazingly useful for making money for their publishers and authors, but obviously quite useless for lessening the number of overweight people. I do not doubt that some people lose weight this way, but the facts are quite clear: the majority of people who buy the books do not. Presumably, their diet problems are caused by things that the diet books do not address. In the same way, the thousands of eager imitators of GE have yet to produce a flood of corporations producing similar results. Copying the mannerisms and dress of, Napoleon, for example, will not make me a world leader (though it might get me a place in a hospital specializing in mental disorders). Trying to act like Jack Welch will not make me a multi-millionaire and a business icon either.

Dealing with dilemmas

Throughout this book, we have explored the various aspects and causes of potential. Inevitably, it has been necessary to take them more or less one at a time. This can lead to the notion that life works that way too. It does not. For any situation more complex than a thirsty person taking a drink of water, there is a whole network of interacting causes and effects taking place simultaneously.

Success in real life is most often a matter of keeping all these elements in some kind of balance. We looked at this earlier under the heading of dysfunctional values and deteriorated strengths. But if we broaden the scale and try to encompass the *Even Bigger Picture*, we can see another area where balance can be hard to find.

Many of our daily problems go beyond matters of balancing strengths or resolving competing values. They arise because we rarely face issues with simple answers like "yes or no" or "pick a choice from this list." Often we do not even have the information we want to allow us to make any choice. Because life is messy and uncertain, we find ourselves having to choose between situations when they are all just about equally attractive or unattractive or plain scary. These are *dilemmas*.

A DILEMMA is a choice that must be made when there are no clear alternatives or no obvious ways of choosing between the ones we can see. It is the desire to put 110 percent into our working lives *and* have plenty of free time to spend with our families and friends. It is being caught between wishing to fit in with the group *and* stand out from all the rest as the best performer. It is feeling damned if we do and damned if we do not.

Dilemmas cannot be solved at the scale where they arise. If our dilemma is based on how we operate within a team, it cannot be resolved within the team. If we are torn between the demands of working life and the demands of home and social life, we cannot resolve that dilemma by looking at the attractions of each of these and attempting to choose between them.

You can only see the way out of dilemma by shifting the scale "upwards" to a wider perspective. Within the team, we may be torn between needing to fit and wanting to stand out. That is insoluble. Whatever we choose, we will miss the other. But if we shift the perspective towards the *Even Bigger Picture* and ask ourselves what will work best for us in the context of, say, the next decade of our working life, the answer may be quite plain. If we want to feel accepted and welcomed amongst a group of friends, we must not do anything to upset the group. If our aspiration is to be CEO, it may make more sense to stand out in almost everything we do, even if it incites envy and even some antagonism.

Real transformation

It is hard to sum up this book's contents in a few sentences. This has been a complex journey through the innermost workings of the human mind. As individuals, we are intricate beings, full of contradictions and complications. The teams and organizations we build share the same characteristics. There are no simple answers to life's problems, at work or at home.

What has, I hope, been clear is that we can either view the reality around us as a minefield or a classroom. The minefield view will encourage us to play safe and avoid going into the unknown. We will stay on the paths we know and concentrate on how to be safe. The classroom perspective will allow us to see today's issues and setbacks as the means to transform ourselves into something new and more fulfilling. We can truly become the best versions of ourselves; triumphantly unique and focused on all our strengths, instead of grappling endlessly with our inevitable weaknesses and shortcomings.

It is our choice. No one can force us to grow and use more of our potential. If it seems too threatening or too difficult, we can choose freely to stand still and live within our present zones of comfort.

You may have encountered this Spanish proverb: "Take what you want," says God "and pay for it." We can take what we want from our lives, safety or excitement. There is always a cost. Choosing safety will cost us much of our potential. We may reach the end of our working days knowing that we could, and should, have done better.

We may find bitterness and frustration are part of the price as well.

Choosing to grow and develop towards our full potential may cost us many bruises, setbacks and downright failures. It will never be comfortable. Other people may find us difficult and demanding. They may prefer not to be our friends. They may compete with us and produce many of the cuts and bruises and broken bones we will suffer.

The rewards will include being able to hold up our heads, knowing that we came to be the best versions of ourselves that we could be. We may find great material success or little. That does not signify much. What matters is that we fulfilled our unique nature, something no one else in the whole sweep of the history of the universe has ever, or will ever, be able to do again. For some of us, that is worth all the pain and more.

Summary

* Meaning is given by and changes with *context*. Without a context that is clearly understood, words or events may be ambiguous or completely unintelligible.
* By changing the context for our experience from our narrow, immediate and local concerns to something much more long-term and inclusive of others, we see events in a new light. Our interpretation of their significance and their meaning usually changes as well.
* There can be several different contexts operating in our lives at the micro level and at the level of the Big Picture. There can be more than one Big Picture, although the number of variants tends to be

small. Big Pictures merge into something still more comprehensive: the *Even Bigger Picture*.

* Possibility is the essence of potential, and a wider perspective gives us a way into unused and unrecognized potential. The *Even Bigger Picture* is the broadest perspective we can access, so it is the place where we can find most possibilities and learning options.
* Confusion about causes and effects is a primary reason for workplace problems. What appears to be a cause from one perspective may turn out to be an effect when we broaden our viewpoint.
* Many of our daily problems arise because we face issues with no simple answers. Dilemmas make us choose between situations that are equally attractive or unattractive and cannot be solved at the scale where they arise. You can only see the way out of dilemma by shifting the scale "upwards" to a wider perspective.
* We can view the reality around us as a minefield or a classroom. The minefield view encourages us to play safe and avoid the unknown. The classroom perspective allows us to see the means to transform ourselves into the best versions of ourselves: to fulfill our potential completely.

SELECT BIBLIOGRAPHY

1. Aftel, Mandy. 1996. **The Story of Your Life: Becoming the Author of Your Experience.** New York: Fireside Books.
2. Argyris, Chris. 1991. **Teaching Smart People How To Learn. Harvard Business Review** (May-June): 5-15.
3. Block, Peter. 1993. **Stewardship: Choosing Service over Self-Interest.** San Francisco: Berrett-Koehler Publishers.
4. -----. 2002. **The Answer to How is Yes.** San Francisco: Berrett-Koehler Publishers.
5. Bohm, David. 1992. **Thought as a System.** New York: Routledge.
6. Branden, Nathaniel. 1997. **Taking Responsibility: Self-reliance and the Accountable Life.** New York: Fireside.
7. -----. 1999. **The Art of Living Consciously.** New York: Fireside Books.
8. Collins, James C. 2001. **Good to Great: Why Some Companies Make the Leap--and Others Don't.** New York, NY: HarperBusiness.
9. -----. 2001. **Level 5 Leadership: The Triumph of Humility and Fierce Resolve. Harvard Business Review** (January): 66-76.
10. Collins, James C., & Porras, Jerry L. 1994. **Built to Last: Successful Habits of Visionary Companies.** New York: Random House.
11. Cooper, Robert K. 2001. **The Other 90%: How to Unlock your Vast Untapped Potential for Leadership and Life.** New York: Crown Business.
12. Csikzentmihalyi, Mihaly. 1990. **Flow: The Psychology of Optimal Experience.** New York: HarperCollins.

13 Deci, Edward L. 1995. **Why We Do What We Do: Understanding Self-Motivation.** New York: Penguin Books.
14 Drucker, Peter F. 1999. **Managing Oneself.** Harvard Business Review (March-April): 65-74.
15 Frankl, Viktor E. 1978. **The Unheard Cry for Meaning.** New York: Washington Square Press.
16 -----. 1984. **Man's Search for Meaning.** New York: Washington Square Press.
17 Gallwey, W. Timothy. 2000. **The Inner Game of Work.** New York: Random House.
18 Harvey, Jerry B. 1999. **How Come Every Time I Get Stabbed in the Back My Fingerprints are on the Knife: and Other Meditations on Management.** San Francisco: Jossey-Bass.
19 Knight, Frank Hyneman. 1921. **Risk, Uncertainty and Profit.** Boston, New York: Houghton Mifflin Company.
20 Schumacher, E.F. 1977. **A Guide for the Perplexed.** New York: Harper & Row.
21 Thomas, Kenneth W. 2000. **Intrinsic Motivation at Work: Building Energy and Commitment.** San Francisco: Berrett-Koehler Publishers.
22 Thompson, C. Michael. 2000. **The Congruent Life: Following the Inward Path to Fulfilling Work and Inspired Leadership.** San Francisco: Jossey-Bass Publishers.
23 Wheatley, Margaret J. 1992. **Leadership and the New Science: Learning about Organization from an Orderly Universe.** San Francisco: Berrett-Koehler Publishers.
24 -----. 2002. **Turning to One Another: Simple Conversations to Restore Hope to the Future.** San Francisco: Berrett-Koehler Publishers, Inc.
25 Zander, Rosamund Stone, & Zander, Benjamin. 2000. **The Art of Possibility.** Boston: Harvard Business Press.

INDEX

Accountability 20, 21
Adaptation .... 15, See also Improvisation
Seed bed of potential 9
Advertising 23
Anger 103–6
Argyris, Chris 78
Aristotle 161
Aspiration 107
Attention 167–69, 179
Focused 175–76
Automatic pilot 26
Automatic responses 39–40, 54, 142, 144, 148–51
Awareness 29–30, 37, 44, 45, 53

Beginner's Mind 135
Beliefs 101–3, 110
Benz, Carl 19
Blockages .... 11, 54, 99, 110, See also Habits
Antidotes 99
Cause and effect 17
Imaginary boundaries 19, 23–24
Inadequate thinking 40–41
Quick fixes 35, 36
Unconscious patterns 100–101

Use of role models *35*
   Buddhists 135
   Burnout 91

   Cause and effect 43–46, 163, 200–202, 206
Underlying structures *95*
   Competence 57, 90
   Concept formation 165–66
   Conscious choice ... 20–21, 26, 39, 41, 44, 48–49, 153–64, 174, 177
Confuse influence and control *41–42*
Increasing it *179*
   Conscious incompetence 181–89
   Context 205
Changes meaning *192*
Creates opportunity *197–200*
Even Bigger Picture *191–206*
Multiple *194–96, 205*
Shifting *194*
   Creating perspective 196–97
   Criticism 24
   Cynicism 82

   Deficit thinking 22, 88, 90, 102
   Delphic Oracle 29
   Depression 108
   Development 109, 131
Probing Questions *133–34*
   Dilemmas 202–4, 206
   Diversity 118–20, 123
   Drucker, Peter 30

Emotions	61
Excitement	87
Experimentation	161
Exploration	53

Faith	75, 76, 82
Based on facts	*77–78*
Fear	124, 131–33, 134, 139
Of Failure	*78*
Flow states	87
Frankl, Viktor	154, 158, 192
Fulfillment	170, 171

Gallwey, Timothy	99
Gifts	*See also* Talents, Strengths
Focusing on	*25*
Going it alone	79
Guilt	108

Habit	26, 141–52
Acts as mental filter	*47*
Confusion about truth	*47–48*
Creates mental fog	*37*
Defensive	*183*
Mental processes	*72–73*
Rigid goals	*59*
Solidified	*145, 149, 152*
Habitual behavior	150
Habitual thinking	69–71
Harvey, Jerry	22
How, More important than what	55

Improvisation .... 10, 15, *See also* Adaptation

Jealousy 106–8

Kick-starting the process 56
Knowledge 34, 46
Learning 9, 92, 159, 163
Need for novelty *93–94, 185*
To access potential *33, 92*
   Living on the edge 137, 139
   Low self-esteem 108

Maps 76, 80
Meaning 205
Mentors 186–89
Momentous choices 158
Motivation 32, 61, 125
Emotional basis *63*
Link to causes *62*

Not knowing 135–37

Obedience 131
Obsession 112, 117, 123
Oedipus 21
Opinions
Taken as truth *136*
   Options 88, 154, 174–75
Limited by habit *155, 158*
   Organizational systems 40

Paths to learning 71

Plato 136, 161
Possibility 25, 26, 88, 125, 130–31, 197, 206
Potential .... 14, 90, *See also* Strengths
Affected by environment *8*
Always expansive *8–9, 14, 54, 94, 96*
Defined *7–8, 10, 13, 14, 30, 86, 159*
Exploration and discovery *17, 35, 58–59, 60, 81–82*
How more important than what *55–56*
Increases satisfaction *96–97*
Indicators of *83–97*
Links to learning *71*
Misunderstood *3–4*
Not special *137*
Realizing it *18–19, 26, 56–57, 126, 155, 160, 163, 165, 178, 182*
Seen as a process *31*
Sources of *32*
Teams and organizations *31–32*
Where to start *13–14, 15, 56, 58, 75*
    Presence of mind 124
    Pythagoras 161

Repetition 92
Responses and reactions 177–78
Restraint 105
Rule Number 6 126

Scarcity 169–72
Scientific method 161–63
Self-loathing 108–10
Self-righteousness 112, 123
Shifting focus 121

213

Short-term perspective 94–95
Slowing down 173–74
Socrates 136
Sophocles 22
Strengths 51, 53, 88, 169
Alignment with values *64*
Deteriorated *111–15*
Knowing them *52–53*
Neglected *89*
Restoring *120–21, 123*
   Stretching 90, 91

Talent 160
Habitual *146*
   Transformation 204–5

Uncertainty 127–30, 138, 139
Different than risk *173*

Values 51, 60, 84
Always right *67, 85*
Automatic basis *64, 67–69*
Core values *93–94, 116*
Dysfunctional *115–18, 119, 123*
Dysfunctional versions *65–66*
Fuel emotions *63, 115*
Matters of the heart *65*
Processes not things *66–67*
Relative *84*
Sources of *66*

Watching ourselves 53

Weaknesses..25, 53, 73
Best forgotten..*54*
Wheatley, Margaret.. 109

Zander, Rosamund and Benjamin............................ 126
Zooming... 122

ABOUT THE AUTHOR

Adrian Savage is president of PNA, Incorporated, based in New Jersey. Educated in England at The Cathedral School, Hereford, and Peterhouse, Cambridge, he is also a Fellow of the Chartered Institute of Personnel and Development. For more than twenty-five years, Mr. Savage has researched the way people and organizations utilize their potential, developing new ways of understanding what allows companies to achieve optimum performance. He has been a consultant to national and multinational businesses on both sides of the Atlantic and a university lecturer, as well as holding senior management positions in several large organizations.

PNA, Incorporated provides organizations with systems and solutions for talent management, organizational development, succession planning and staff retention. It also helps many executive coaches to deepen their work with key individuals by adding the dimension of exploring unutilized potential. Clients include major corporations, consulting networks and governments. Using proprietary approaches developed and proven over more than fifteen years, PNA helps national and international clients maximize individual, team and organizational strengths to achieve their business goals. PNA is part of the global RSM International network, the eighth largest business services operation in the world.

Visit www.nettps.com for more information or call 908.541.1700.